Unrequited Love and Gay Latino Culture

Unrequited Love and Gay Latino Culture

What Have You Done to My Heart?

BY

Daniel T. Contreras

UNREQUITED LOVE AND GAY LATINO CULTURE
© Daniel T. Contreras, 2005.

All rights reserved. No part of this book may be used or reproduced in any manner whatsoever without written permission except in the case of brief quotations embodied in critical articles or reviews.

First published in 2005 by
PALGRAVE MACMILLAN™
175 Fifth Avenue, New York, N.Y. 10010 and
Houndmills, Basingstoke, Hampshire, England RG21 6XS.
Companies and representatives throughout the world.

PALGRAVE MACMILLAN is the global academic imprint of the Palgrave Macmillan division of St. Martin's Press, LLC and of Palgrave Macmillan Ltd. Macmillan® is a registered trademark in the United States, United Kingdom and other countries. Palgrave is a registered trademark in the European Union and other countries.

ISBN 1–4039–6468–8 hardback

Library of Congress Cataloging-in-Publication Data

Contreras, Daniel.
   Unrequited love and gay latino culture : What have you done to my heart? / Daniel Contreras.
     p. cm.
   Includes bibliographical references and index.
   ISBN 1–4039–6468–8
    1. Popular culture—United States. 2. Arts, American—20th century. 3. Love in literature. 4. Suffering in literature. 5. United States—Social life and customs—1971– I. Title.

E169.04.C665 2004
306'.0973—dc22   2004049789

A catalogue record for this book is available from the British Library.

Design by Newgen Imaging Systems (P) Ltd., Chennai, India.

First edition: January 2005

10 9 8 7 6 5 4 3 2 1

Printed in the United States of America.

Contents

Acknowledgments   vii

Introduction: "What Have You Done to My Heart?":
Unrequited Love and The Question of Utopia   1

1. *The Boys in the Band*: Camp and the Heartbreak
of Race   23

2. "Letting Go of What you Love": Literature,
Popular Culture, and Chicano Heartache   51

3. Utopian Drag and Gender Politics   75

4. Kiss: Utopian Romance and Manuel Puig's Spider Woman   99

Conclusion: *Somewhere Better Than This Place/
Nowhere Better Than This Place*   131

References   137
Index   143

Acknowledgments

This book would not have been possible without the support and the love of Ryan H. Carmichael who worked harder on getting this to press than anyone else, even me. To him I owe more than this book can repay.

I would like to thank The Modern Thought and Literature Program at Stanford University where I was given the space and freedom to explore my initial ideas about this theme. My advisors, Ramon Saldívar, Renato Rosaldo, and Yvonne Yarbro Bejarano supported the project and let me know it was worth pursuing. I have known Ramon since my undergraduate days at University of Texas, Austin and his example of scholarship and political commitment, while daunting, have always inspired me. Renato believed so much in this work when I had so much doubt that I must thank him again.

The ideas in the book began while I was at Stanford, especially when Richard Dyer visited for a seminar. His work and ensuing friendship have meant the world to me.

I would like to thank Ardel Thomas for her friendship all these years. Monica Moore at MTL helped me through various bumps along the academic road, so thank you.

My friends in San Francisco, Jose Salazar and David Richardson, taught me a lot about friendship and loyalty and that rough times don't mean you can't have fun.

Of course, I must thank my parents, Ninfa and Ted, who believed in me from the start and kept on believing. I would like to thank my sister Uma with whom I shared many ideas from this book.

Thanks to everyone in the English Department at Colby College for taking me in so warmly. Especially, Jenny Boylan for support and Cedric Bryant, Katherine Stubbs, and Pat Onion for "discovering me." Thanks to Judy Daviau for helping me so much in the final stages and to Jennifer Thorn for her guidance and generous perspicacity.

At the risk of sentimentality, I must thank Ryan again for his love and care—what a gift!

Introduction: "What Have You Done to My Heart?": Unrequited Love and The Question of Utopia

The title of this book refers to the jazz standard "April in Paris," composed by E. Y. Harburg and Vernon Duke, here as sung by Ella Fitzgerald and Louis Armstrong. "What have you done to my heart?" is the last line of the song, expressing the heartbreak associated with the beauty of Paris in the spring, seen through the vivid context of a broken love affair. Within the line is a commingling of romantic yearning and remembrance, and this project partakes in this ambiance. I also want the lyric to function as a refrain throughout the work in this sense: popular culture has impacted various communities and various people (myself included) in profoundly emotional and strangely moving ways. Popular culture has indeed done something to my heart—it has given my emotions a context and a history. The line also contains a recognition that this change in the heart is irreversible. A transformation is effected, which is experienced—at the same time—as a gift and as a mourned loss. There is, too, an ironic juxtaposition in combining the smooth, silky voice of Ella Fitzgerald, who was famous for her sensuous and perfect pitch, with Louis Armstrong's gruff, idiosyncratic one. This odd, yet somehow "just right" kind of juxtaposition is emblematic of what I explore throughout this book.

In many different ways, this project, from its title to its sensibility, was conceptualized through Ella Fitzgerald, particularly her sumptuous 1950s Verve recordings. When Fitzgerald signed on with Norman Granz in 1950, Granz envisioned an epic recording project: Fitzgerald would record the Great American Songbook. Each of the great composers of the 1930s, including George Gershwin, Cole Porter, Rodgers & Hart, and Harold Arlen would be featured in a "Songbook" album, with Fitzgerald's distinctive fidelity to the lyrics and music.

The albums achieved lasting fame for Fitzgerald, and it was these records, and this period in her career, that ensured her place in American popular culture.

I discovered these recordings during my first year of graduate school at Stanford University, when I had already begun thinking seriously about questions of sentimentality and sensibility, especially through the historical context of Chicano culture. Mexican American culture has invested heavily in representations of suffering, both in a Catholic context and in a romantic sense with songs and depictions of intense loss and longing. This has always fascinated me, and I am curious to investigate why such images of despair are so popular and widespread. I especially am interested in unraveling "common sense" and stereotypical notions of this attachment to suffering.

These stereotypes are compounded when considering the question of queer culture and its (commonsensical) investment in the melodramatic, the emotionally excessive, the diva, or in a word, camp. Camp as a concept, a sensibility, an idea, seems to neatly encapsulate what I find most compelling in various texts. I am consistently drawn to books, movies, and songs that depict instances of emotional distress. Often these representations seem exaggerated and even comical; to me, they make a lot of sense.

It seems fitting to consider Latino melodramatic culture with queer camp, since they both operate from historically marginalized spaces. Broadly speaking, one emerged from the colonization of the Americas, the other from the nearly universal stigmatization of homosexuality. Of course, it is important to factor in the very real material differences between racial domination and homophobia, but also, fascinating to consider the overlap and the dialogue between the two. I would like to do this by closely considering instances of suffering in love in literary and dramatic texts.

The other part of my title outlines in broad strokes the historical groundwork of my investigation: that of a racialized desire taking place in a context of unrequited love. I analyze literary, theatrical, and cinematic texts which utilize and incorporate popular culture and these texts' attachment to aspirations for some type of "utopia." Here, I use utopia to designate less of a strictly "political" construction and more of a site in which love, even queer love, is allowed to thrive. Utopia for me marks where impossible loves become inevitably possible. My consideration of utopia *is*, however, "political" in that it uses feeling and desire to revolutionary effect in how it transforms the intimate and the private.

This book investigates specific affective textual investments that circulate in narratives about suffering. The texts that I have chosen may be less historically chronological than culturally topographic. In this work, a popular history, a novel, an artwork, a song, or a movie (all of which receive attention here) will often contain the thematic of a fruitless or unhappy search for "true love." If it seems ludicrous, if not absurd, that mass culture could produce such an intense outburst of feeling, it may prove a bit more plausible if we now examine an art work which holds as its central premise the vital importance of these types of odd, even "junky" joinings, which the artist describes as "colic couplings."

"El Limite" and Colic Coupling

"El Limite" (1991) is a photo installation piece by Celia Alvarez Muñoz, a Chicana artist from El Paso. Through the use of photography and text, Alvarez Muñoz often presents enigmatic and challenging works about Chicano history. I first saw this piece in 1992 in the monumental exhibition, *Chicano Art: Resistance and Affirmation, 1965–1985*. What was evident from the exhibition was the importance of the visual arts to the Chicano Movement, when artwork was produced with explicit political aims in a period of intense collective action and possibility. This lent the show a certain pathos, for it captured a moment, however nostalgically conceived, in which art, politics, and everyday life were seamlessly integrated. The pathos surrounding the show may also have come from the clear demarcation of the show's parameters—the show "ends" in 1985. The implication was clear: the Chicano Movement, as such, was over.

The title of the installation, "El Limite," refers to the limit or maximum cargo load a railroad can carry and the artist describes it as being about "limits with us; the limits we set." She says that the installation is about a toy train: "I'm taking a very simple model of transportation to elucidate a vehicle. What is a vehicle? What vehicle prepares you for life? The toy train was made by Dad. I had him reconstruct it the way he made it when he was a kid. His markings are there. He numbered the cars crudely, with crayons or something" (Jarmusch C–1). The piece consists of two huge photographic scanner murals on cloth. Both are in black and white and depict a train set improvised out of discarded cans and junkyard debris, pictured alongside a written childhood memory. The first text reads:

> Stories by Dad came from two sources: invented
> And real life adventures.
> At times hard to separate or
> Distinguish.

> En Las Arenas near the railroad tracks, they played with toys made out of things that don't belong together. Like combinations we were Warned against.
> Nunca, never, eat watermelon during a certain time.
> Of the month.
> Nunca tome leche cuando come pescado.
> Nunca tome un helado cuando agitado.

The other photograph has this text:

> Some stories stemmed from trips to the Golden State on trains
> Jumped on in El Paso during the Depression years. My favorite
> Stories dealt with the War when he was moved across
> The world and throughout Europe, again,
> Mostly by train.
> Little do we know colic couplings may well become the main
> Ingredients required to Survive.

Each of the photographs is in a wide-screen format, suggestive of a movie screen, and they have decorative corners, which suggest snapshots in a photo album. The contrasting size of a movie screen projection and a small intimate photo reflect on the work's intersecting of the epic and the private. The photographs are placed on two opposite walls at right angles, so as to resemble pages in an open book. Satellite images on the wall accompany the installation, referring to photography and its relationship to the Mexican Revolutionary War. These images include a *soldadera* (a female soldier from the Revolution), an image of a photojournalist documenting the Revolution with the aid of two Indians, and an illustration by Jose Guadalupe Posada depicting a train derailment.

The work's subject matter—displacement and war—is sharply contrasted with the artist's specific childhood memory. But in the guise of this personal, even sweet memory, Alvarez Muñoz offers some conceptual dynamite. Her metaphoric story takes place in the context of global war, and here she knowingly blows up many assumptions about personal experience that rest on powerful, yet ultimately shakable binaries: domestic/public; stable, idyllic community/disruptive, explosive Diaspora; imaginary, memory/real, history.

The Art of Junk

But if "progress" had become inseparable from the process of "development," "capitalism" became a site of intense ambiguity and tension. Fredric Jameson captures this in Marx himself:

> In a well-known passage, Marx powerfully urges us to do the impossible . . . a type of thinking that would be capable of grasping the demonstrably

baleful features of capitalism along with its extraordinary and liberating dynamism simultaneously within a single thought ... We are somehow to lift our minds to a point at which it is possible to understand that capitalism is at one and the same time the best thing that has ever happened to the human race—and the worst. (47)

Jameson's language is about uplifting ideals—the "well known passage" he refers to is from Marx and Engel's *The Communist Manifesto*. This linking of "liberating dynamism" with unrelenting exploitation becomes the grounding "colic coupling" of the artwork. It will also serve as a guiding metaphor for this book, in my endeavor to link what is most abject, with what is most valued, and what is sentimentally trivial with what is crucially important for survival.

Even though a period of extreme economic and social misery, the Great Depression emerges in the artwork as a time of freedom and exploration. The artist's father would "jump trains" to go west, toward the most mythical of places in the national and global imagination, California. World War II was a catastrophic event, causing mass disruption, misery, and death, but the war also created conditions for long lasting social transformations and irrevocably challenged gender and racial conventions. It is also suggested through the artwork that it was this war that placed her father on a global stage.

The perspective this gave the Chicana/o community—the stories the artist heard about her father's experience for example—enabled the capacity to see oneself as part of a world, and being able to act in it, to change it. This perspective also suggests that maybe there is no "Limite" to what we can carry with us, and no limit to how we can transform the conditions around us, regardless of how oppressive. Here the enlargement of toy trains made of junk into epic size photographs metaphorically enlarges the "smallest" (in this case a Chicano) experience into epic size proportions. The trivial aspects of everyday life reveal much of the hidden, obscured relations of society and lend the work poignancy around such resourcefulness. The working-class "strategy" of creating toys out of throwaway junk is placed into a context of social disruption where invention can make anything happen and where the unexpected result is reinscribed as inevitable.

Where this project is concerned, the literal reclaiming of junk provides the tools to imagine reclaiming other throwaway and "trashy" aspects of everyday consumerist life. The "junkiness" of sappy sentiment, the derivative plots of soap operas and Hollywood movies, the aching, masochistic torch songs of betrayal and loss become powerful objects of transformation. To consider castoff objects and experiences in this way is to acknowledge the historical processes lying dormant in materials around us in everyday life. If a "worthless" object can provoke strong emotional attachments it can release a type of surplus value which can be illustrative of the larger workings of power—and resistances to it. What I describe as a "utopian impulse" is, however, mediated by the objects and historical conditions at hand. As Richard Dyer explains in a discussion on images and their reception by various audiences:

> In stressing complexity and contradictories at the point of reception, however, I am not suggesting that people can make representations mean anything they want them to mean. We are all restricted by both the viewing and the reading codes to which we have access (by virtue of where we are situated in the world and in the social order) and by what representations there are for us to view and read. The prestige of high culture, the centralization of mass cultural production, the literal poverty of marginal cultural production: these are aspects of the power relations of representation that put the weight of control over representation on the side of the rich, the white, the male, the heterosexual. Acknowledging the complexity of viewing/reading practices in relation to representation does not entail the claim that there is equality and freedom in the regime of representation. (1992: 3)

In this case, to forget this is to forget that while the artist's father is inventively making toys out of garbage, other children are playing with expensive shiny toys, and their fathers are controlling their large-scale counterparts and waging a war. In the larger scope of this project, I must emphasize that the impulse of wanting to extract something meaningful out of abjection is not to embrace marginality and unfulfillment, nor is it necessarily a clear and total resistance against domination. It may instead be a realistic response to less than ideal circumstances, which may or may not enable the imagining of different realities.

It is important to also place Alvarez Muñoz's installation into an art historical context. While the work is situated formally as a Conceptual artwork, it draws fruitfully upon Dada and Surrealism in its uses and juxtapositions of unlikely objects. Dada, as a European art and literary movement, was a response to the bloody insanity of World War I; Surrealism wanted to visualize the hidden (subconscious) currents of illogic of the "rational" world. These movements were deeply historical at their core and teach us to see the "everyday" as containing important nuggets of historical truth.

The artist's father played with "toys made out of things that don't belong together," which parallels the colic coupling of the other panel. If the binary between "invented" and "real life" is contrasted with the second sentence, we have "invented toy trains" and "real railroad tracks." Dad's real life adventures on real trains becomes as important to the artist as his invented stories on invented toy trains. This is highlighted by the giant image of the improvised toy train. This is not a picture of the train on which her father traveled to the Golden State or throughout Europe, yet it is the one that clearly has the most resonance for the artist.

Importantly, the playfulness of the piece and the central importance of toys to the artist's concept keep pleasure in the periphery of the artwork's dimensions. Indeed, "play" is very serious business in the piece, both as a literal theme, and as its central metaphor. The gentle warnings expressed suggest combinations that perhaps might never have occurred to anyone. As parental warnings, one is assured that they will be ignored, although the results of doing so are not too dire. They are expressed in Chicano fashion, combining English and Spanish, and this switching into another language in the middle of a sentence becomes another "combination we were warned against."

In fact, an example of a colic coupling may be a Chicano—born of two nations, a product of Diaspora, war, genocide, and displacement. For me, the search for "real" and "authentic" roots is difficult, if not impossible, but it does lend a certain poignancy to these searches. The fact that any search for one's home place, for one's community, for one's site of love, will probably, and even necessarily, end in frustration does not mean the search itself does not have its own rewards. Perhaps Alvarez Muñoz is suggesting through the claim that colic couplings are the "key to survival," that it is the "queer," that it is in the "borderlands" (in all senses of the word), that it is out of worthless junk that we can begin to construct a useful utopian geography. And if postmodernism has fragmented all absolutes, such as history, progress, identity, and politics, "colic couplings" may be an image in which we can rethink and remake postmodern despair.

Postmodernism and Affect

One characteristic of postmodernism we shall encounter throughout this project is that postmodernism exists and describes itself as a *list* of cultural phenomena with a series of references from both high and low culture. In fact, Dick Hebdige describes the difficulty of defining postmodernism as it "gets stretched in all directions across different debates, different disciplinary and discursive boundaries, as different factions seek to make it their own, using it to designate a plethora of incommensurable objects, tendencies, emergencies." He then goes on to list some of these:

> The decor of a room, the design of a building, the diegesis of a film, the construction of a record, or a "scratch" video, a TV commercial, or an arts documentary, or the "intertextual" relations between them, the layout of a page in fashion magazine or critical journal, an anti-teleological tendency with epistemology, the attack on the "metaphysics of presence," a general attenuation of feeling, the collective chagrin and morbid projections of a post-war generation of Baby Boomers confronting middle-age, the "predicament" of reflexivity, a group of theoretical tropes, a proliferation of surfaces, a new phase in commodity fetishism, a fascination for "images," codes and styles, a process of cultural, political, or existential fragmentation and/or crisis, the "de-centering" of the subject, and "incredulity towards meta-narratives," the replacement of unitary power axes by a pluralism of power-discourse formation, the "implosion of meaning," the collapse of cultural hierarchies, the dread engendered by the threat of nuclear self-destruction, the decline of the university, the functioning and effects of the new miniaturized technologies, broad societal and economic shifts into a "media," "consumer" or multinational phase. (174)

I cite Hebdige's list in full not only because we will encounter many such lists throughout our investigation, but also because despite the comedy of reading such a vast array of phenomena, the accumulation of them attempts to get at the most slippery of historical locations, "contemporary culture." By extension, that may mean that postmodernism as such simply refers to what is perceived as contemporary American life. Or in fact, it may signal, as Andrew Ross puts it, one of "postmodernism's most provocative lessons; that terms are by no means guaranteed their meaning, and that these meanings can be appropriated and redefined for different purposes, different contexts, and more important, different causes" (xi). That identity can have different "purposes" is an integral and vexing characteristic of contemporary cultural politics. Postmodernism can function to suspend any general assumptions that can be made about "community" or "identity."

My concentration will be on the question of race and racial identity in their varied thematics, but there are certain things this project will not be able to do and subjectivities and concerns even within its specific realm for which it cannot presume to speak. It may seem problematic or limiting to emphasize any particular identity as a space in which to begin, but in a project that is invested in how it is that particular subjects make sense of loss, of racism, of homophobia, it is essential to demarcate the aims and limitations of this investigation. Here I will negotiate between the macropolitics and histories that have produced this marginalization, and the micropolitics of response to this domination.

It is my intention not to write a script in which gay people or people of color are continually defeated in their attempts at empowerment, and I will not look at texts so as to expose the futility of resistance. But neither will I look at texts to prove that this resistance is always present and successful. I will instead concentrate on the uses of popular culture, especially in its expression of "affect." As Lawrence Grossberg describes it in his book *We Gotta Get Out of This Place: Popular Conservatism and Postmodern Culture*, "Popular culture seems to work at the intersection of the body and emotions. Emotion is itself a notoriously difficult topic for cultural critics who often try to explain it as if it were merely the aura of ideological effects . . . Affect is perhaps the most difficult plane of human life to define and describe . . . because there is no critical vocabulary to describe its different form and structures" (79).

The Borderlands and Queer Culture

If I choose to think through a notoriously difficult concept, that of affect and popular culture, I do so in a challenging framework—that of thinking through race and sexuality simultaneously. One essential text in exploring questions of race and sexuality is Gloria Anzaldua's 1987 book, *Borderlands: La Frontera, The New Mestiza*. Anzaldua's book has since been taken up in various ways both in and out of the academy, but it perhaps found its most potent influence in women's studies, and academic feminism in general. In the book, the Borderlands is represented as a "vague and undetermined place created by the emotional residue of an unnatural boundary. It is in a constant state of transition. The prohibited and forbidden are its inhabitants . . . the squint-eyed, the perverse, the queer, the troublesome, the mongrel, the mulatto, the half-breed, the half dead; in short, those who cross over, pass over, or go through the confines of the 'normal' " (Anzaldua 3). Anzaldua's Borderlands offer a postmodern context and a compelling image with its ambiguity about totality and not smoothing over rough edges. For feminists, her work offered a strong indictment of a middle-class feminism that was unwilling or unable to accommodate not only those outside of its white racial parameters, but those outside of its heterosexual, bourgeois politics. Indeed, Anzaldua's use of "queer" itself anticipated the formation of Queer Theory's central axioms.

In trying to elaborate what queerness can mean, Eve Kosofsky Sedgwick writes: "Things that queer can refer to: the open mesh of possibilities, gaps, overlaps, dissonances and resonances, lapses and excess of meaning when the constituent elements of anyone's gender, of anyone's sexuality aren't made (or can't be made) to signify monolithically" (8). It is this queer sexuality situated in the Borderlands that proves so politically and creatively productive for many gay people of color. It is similarly potent that "queer" as different, as not "mainstream" or "normal," becomes intensely sexual. The transgression of norms generates an erotic and passionate energy that informs, in my opinion, the most interesting of queer projects.

Sedgwick discusses the idea of "queer" further:

> A lot of the most exciting work around "queer" spins the term outward along dimensions that can't be subsumed under gender and sexuality at all: the ways that race, ethnicity, postcolonial nationality criss-cross with these and other identity-constituting identity fracturing discourses, for example. Intellectuals and artists of color whose sexual self-definition includes "queer"—I think of an Isaac Julien, a Gloria Anzaldua. (9)

Throughout Sedgwick's work, she continually prizes the queer moments in texts and culture in which "the richest junctures weren't the ones where everything means the same thing" (6). In fact, Sedgwick sees cultural workers such as Anzaldua using the "leverage of 'queer' to do a new kind of justice to the fractal intricacies of language, skin, migration, state. Thereby, the gravity (I mean the gravitas, the meaning, but also the center of gravity) of the term 'queer' itself deepens and shifts" (9). That Sedgwick locates intense productive possibilities in fractured identities provides a powerful influence on this project, as does Anzaldua's work on the dislocations of living on borders.

In fact, what is intensely exciting for many of us who actually were born and raised in Anzaldua's Borderlands—the generally impoverished border region of South Texas—is to consider this area as "queer." The history of migration of Chicanos throughout the entire Southwest and beyond in search of work and economic sustenance is relatively well documented (if not overly valued in "official" accounts of U.S. history). What is much less researched is the experience of those queer Chicanos who could not wait to leave their birthplace in search of sexual and emotional freedom: those narratives of achievement, of acquiring scholarships to study far away, of seeking professional employment in urban areas away from what was seen as unbearably oppressive homophobia, or the narratives of leaving with nothing, and making the best life one can, far from home, but free to pursue some type of emotional fulfillment. As Cherrie Moraga writes, "I gradually became Anglocized because I thought it was the only option available to me toward gaining autonomy as a person without being sexually stigmatized . . . I instinctively made choices which I though would allow me greater freedom of movement in the future" (99). But this experience of leaving, of losing some part of the self, is never seamless, or complete.

Just as Anzaldua writes her book from Northern California, having long "gone west," the melancholy of leaving infuses many gay texts. The queer Chicano can place "exile" in a historical trajectory of movement; it is in this movement and displacement that we can begin to consider the complexity of this estrangement. In fact, Anzaldua tells a story of teaching in a New England college where she and three other lesbians met with a group of heterosexual students and faculty who were disconcerted by their presence. One of the students remarks, "I thought homophobia meant fear of going home after a residency." Anzaldua comments on this pun: "And I thought, how apt. We're afraid of being abandoned by the mother, the culture, *la Raza*, for being unacceptable, faulty, damaged. Most of us unconsciously believe that if we reveal this unacceptable aspect of the self our mother/culture/race will totally reject us" (20). This fear of rejection makes it difficult to reconcile the volatile combination of race and sexuality; they often mark a conflict that tends to wipe out traces of the other, leaving a residue of the self.

One of the most powerful chapters in *Borderlands* is entitled "How to Tame a Wild Tongue." It begins with the striking image of Anzaldua getting her teeth cleaned. The dentist's first words are, "We're going to have to control your tongue" (53). As he tries to keep Anzaldua's tongue down while cleaning her teeth, he says in exasperation, "I've never seen anything as strong or as stubborn." Anzaldua writes, "And I think, how do you tame a wild tongue, train it to be quiet, how do you bridle and saddle it? How do you make it lie down?" (53). From the sterile, modern context of a dentist chair, Anzaldua begins musing about language and remembers being "caught speaking Spanish at recess—that was good for three licks on the knuckles with a sharp ruler." The speaking of a language is then never afforded an innocence; she describes her experiences as a Chicana in South Texas and how the prohibition of Spanish by Anglos was not the only battle. In fact, she writes, "Chicano Spanish is considered by the purist and by most Latinos as deficient, a mutilation of Spanish" (55). Anzaldua describes Chicanos as a "people who are neither Spanish nor live in a country in which Spanish is the first language . . . a people who live in a country in which English is the reigning tongue but who are not Anglo . . . a people who cannot entirely identify with either standard (formal, Castilian) Spanish nor standard English." She then makes a compelling point, "What recourse is left to them but to create their own language?" (55).

Indeed, what other recourse could there be? This inventiveness and this will to survive in the face of cultural annihilation is also part of the power of living on the borderlands, of living in the space of "queerness," to be that which doesn't quite fit. Anzaldua does not romanticize this space and carefully and often painfully describes the violence in this repression. She sees power behind the mixing of borders, however, and describes a "malleability that renders us unbreakable, we, the mestizas and mestizos" (64). This "malleability" is an important image for thinking through the kinds of cultural productions I will be discussing, some Chicano and some not, but all concerning those on the Borderlands of society.

Searching, Moving, Desire

That searches for a type of utopia are always doomed does not negate the meaningfulness of those searches or what they can produce. In my readings of various texts, I will be following this trajectory of moving, of searching. In this, I am partly drawing on Peter Brooks' *Reading for the Plot*, where he explores exactly what plot is in literary texts and how it achieves a particular and specific dynamism within a text. Brooks writes, "Plot itself—narrative design and intention—is the figure of displacement, desire leading to change of position . . . Desire necessarily becomes textual by way of a specifically narrative impulse, since desire is metonymy, a forward drive in the signifying chain, an insistence of meaning toward the occulted objects of desire" (84). This forward drive is far from straightforward:

> Narrative sequences and scenarios must accord with the complex, twisting, and subversive patterning of desire. The insistent past must be allowed to write its design at the same time one attempts to unravel it. As well as having form, plots must generate force: the force that makes the connection of incidents powerful, that shapes the confused material of a life into an intentional structure that in turn generates new insights about how life can be told. (282)

Significantly, Brooks sees narratives as possessing a force, as always containing some type of quest narrative, that may or may not be frustrated in its outcome. He also sees the potency in various forms: "It is also that we grasp here the power of narrative, even the lurid melodramatic fictional narrative, to generate narrative, and the power of reading to illuminate not merely the text read but other texts of everyday life as well, creating new possibilities of meaning in the world" (165). The "desire" that Brooks invokes is psychoanalytically inflected, but, while not wanting to minimize the importance and even centrality of this interpretation, I will place "desire" more effectively for my purposes as "affect."

Grossberg characterizes "desire" as implying a purely, or at least primarily, libidinal and sexual aspect, which focuses on a particular object. "Affect," Grossberg argues, "actually points to a complex set of effects which circulate around notions of investment and anchoring . . . Affect identifies the strength of the investment which anchors people in particular experiences, practices, identities, meanings, and pleasures . . ." The task then is finding sites of meaning and investment that exist in culture for various audiences (for example, gays and lesbians and/or people of color), and historically locating these sites in as complex a field as possible (82–85).

But to discuss the affective qualities of popular culture, something so ephemeral and filled with individual, subjective meaning, seems to call for a psychoanalytic framework of some type. While I would not want my project to seem either hostile to or ignorant of psychoanalytic discourses, its parameters will generally close off any in-depth critical use of its conceptual tools. Instead, I will rely upon Richard Dyer's work on popular culture, such as his book *Only Entertainment* in which he describes what he sees as psychoanalysis' generally "negative view of pleasure" and its "preference for the words 'pleasure' and 'desire'" (4). Dyer's concern is that psychoanalysis and much academic criticism looks through entertainment and popular culture without paying much attention to what exactly is entertaining about it, or what function it could be playing in the culture at large. Dyer sees the negative view of entertainment as being part of the:

> . . . broadly left discussion of entertainment, even when it is not pychoanalytically inclined. Some of this discussion takes the time-honored view of entertainment as the sugar on the pill of the real meaning and purpose of the cultural product in question, which in this case is "ideology." Whether canvassing the need for the left to use entertainment forms as the vector to reach the mass of the people, condemning the

dominant ideology for its unabashed recourse to entertainment for the promulgation of existing class, gender and race relations, or joining the two in (rightly) characterizing entertainment as a site of ideological struggle, such accounts in general take what the sugar is as unproblematic. (5)

That's Entertainment

Drawing upon Dyer's concerns, I will be attentive to the specific things that popular culture does (and does not do) and its myriad effects on specific audiences, rather than trying to conjure up the best possible political interpretations. This also calls for attentiveness to the contextual arenas that texts inhabit. This book investigates various affective investments, or better, particular attachments, that certain characters or subjects hold tightly. For example, whether in popular history, a novel, a play, or a movie, through various "colic couplings" of race and sexuality, the texts discussed will often contain the thematic of a search for "true love," and, not at all coincidentally, this will often be mediated through Hollywood movies. This should not be too surprising, for as Dyer notes, it is entertainment that "teaches us enjoyment . . . it works with the desires that circulate in a given society at a given time, neither wholly constructing those desires nor merely reflecting desire produced elsewhere; it plays a major role in the social construction of happiness" (7).

One trap that an investigation such as this can fall into is that of ahistoricity. To talk about emotion, to talk about affective investments, to talk about love or happiness, is often to generalize and universalize (not to mention sentimentalize). I see the discussion of love and emotion in queer popular culture as a productive and political project. As Grossberg argues:

> In fact, affect is the missing term in an adequate understanding of ideology, for it offers the possibility of a "psychology of belief" . . . It is the affective investment in particular ideological sites (which may or may not be libidinal or nonlibidinal) that explains the power of the articulation which bonds particular representations and realities . . . The dominance of the affective dimension does not mean that such popular formulations do not also involve relations of ideology and pleasure, materiality and economics . . . Popular culture, operating within an affective sensibility is a crucial ground where people give others, whether cultural practices or social groups the authority to shape their identity and locate them within various circuits of power. By making certain things matter, people "authorize" them to speak for them, not only as a spokesperson but also as a surrogate voice. People give authority to that which they invest in; they let them organize their emotional and narrative life and identity. (84)

These affective investments, these things that "matter" to particular clusters of people, are important for understanding how to make progressive politics in a postmodern context. As Grossberg puts it, "Affective empowerment is increasingly important in a world in which pessimism has become common sense, in which people increasingly feel incapable of making a difference... Affective relations are, at least potentially, the condition of possibility for the optimism, invigoration and passion which are necessary for any struggle to change the world. At this level, popular culture offers the resources, which may or may not be mobilized into forms of popular struggle, resistance, and opposition" (86). I want to offer a workable framework for making sense of specific aspects of popular culture and entertainment. That this framework is decidedly queer, and heavily coated with racial speculations, will necessarily limit its scope; what I hope will not be limited is its ability to reframe other questions and concerns.

To write about the effects and uses of popular culture, or "entertainment," seems always to be about negotiating blind optimism and glaring historical and material conditions. In my case, the critic wants to be able to analytically grasp the "object" of study, whether it be a song, a movie, a play, and make it perform political magic. And, more often than not, it is the critic's own investments that lend the subject/object of attention its importance and primacy.

"To requite" is to pay back in kind, and using this economic notion deliberately, especially as we talk of "investments," this work explores various kinds of unrequited relationships. The progressive, even radical ideologies we might hold—whether nationalism, Marxism, gay liberation, feminism—cannot always keep their promises. Similarly, to invest in the liberatory power of popular culture is to be continually disappointed by its constant co-option by corporate power, to be dismayed by its reactionary narratives and obsessions, and to be frustrated by its often placidly passive (at best) response to political and historical crisis. The critic, through all this, of course, becomes finally implicated in, what at its most ideal can only be described as, political ambivalence. Yet we don't want to give up on popular culture or on liberatory political theory; and these investments are a strong negation of the despair of contemporary popular and political culture. The sense of being drawn back again and again to the hegemonic struggle and to the indeterminacy of postmodern political and social life, is at one level to believe, and to admit, that the unrequited relationship is not a futile one and that it contains its own share of pleasures and possibilities. To experience unrequited love is above all to feel keenly and unmistakably the sting of unfulfilled desires. But this sting is produced by that very desire for something ideal, something wonderful, something impossible, something utopian.

Stuart Hall writes, "The metaphor of the discursive, of textuality, instantiates a necessary delay, a displacement which I think is always implied in the concept of culture. If you work on culture, or if you've tried to work on some other really important things and you find yourself driven back to culture, if culture happens to be what seizes hold of your soul, you have to recognize that you will always be working in an area of displacement..." (271). Here it is "culture" which has seized me and consequently has forced a displacement. If I know—intellectually and intuitively—that the study of culture involves close study of something ephemeral and ultimately, ambivalent, I also know it has done something to my heart. What exactly it has done is at the core of this book. I have a strong interest in exploring the potentialities of unrequited love as a form of recovery: if we don't mine something of value in the disappointment and pain, then all is surely lost. What I argue throughout is that all is not lost in loss; often what we lose in life can be recovered in art; I wonder, too, whether that recovery can have other effects outside of its immediate sphere.

Personal Narrative

Much of the inspiration for this investigation can be found in my relationship to Hollywood and how it has intertwined in my emotional life. Movies provided a utopian vision of possibilities of the heart and secured for me a belief in the power of fantasy. When I was very young, I was terrified of movies and of movie theaters. I remember my parents taking me to some children's film (*Pufnstuf*), when I was three or four years old and being in the theater, cowering. I was fascinated and thrilled and scared out of my wits. The darkness, the deep red curtains, the flickering lights and shadows suggested something sinister and unknown. It was a sense of unreality, something dreamlike, and also a sense of being out of control—that the senses could be manipulated in mysterious, perhaps unwanted ways. Pauline Kael writes:

> Movies—which arouse special, private, hidden feelings—have always had an erotic potential... This was obviously a factor in the early disapproval of movies, even if it wasn't consciously formulated. Probably movies weren't culturally responsible for such a long time because they are so sheerly enjoyable; in a country with a Puritan background, the

sensuality of movies was bound to be suspect . . . Movies can overwhelm us, as no other art form does . . . For some people being carried away by a movie is very frightening: not everyone wants to have many senses affected at once. (*Reeling* xi)

Movies did hold a strong power over me and it was irresistible. They brought out what I was just then beginning to recognize and name as the "emotional." In fact, it was from movies that I would learn to feel—to begin to design what I thought "love" was, or what a "relationship" should look like.

While I was about five or six years old, growing up in hot, boring Brownsville, Texas on the United States/Mexico border, every Saturday my cousins and I would go to the "Mexico" theater (that is what it was called) where my Tia Hela worked the box office. My aunt never married, and she was very vain. I remember watching her get ready for work, and she would literally take hours, doing her hair, her makeup, her outfits. She was a movie star without a movie that worked at the theater daintily pushing steel buttons releasing cardboard tickets. Since Brownsville is always hot and blindingly sunny, we would spend all afternoon in the cool air-conditioned darkness watching double features of Mexican movies. I have read pieces by Chicanos and Latinos describing their childhood initiation into classic Mexican cinema and its glamorous stars, Maria Felix, Dolores del Rio, and others. These were not the movies we saw. I was introduced to the cinema by Mexican B-Movie classics about wrestlers and monsters like *Las Vampiras* with Mil Mascaras. In fact, horror movies and films having anything to do with the supernatural have always fascinated me, and to this day, when I am visiting my family, my father and I will duck into a theater to watch any trashy, scary movie playing.

Movies remained important to me through my adolescence. Both my parents worked, so my grandmother would take care of me after school, and it was from her that I received my most profound and lasting gift, my love of melodramatic narrative. We would talk about all the *telenovelas* and soap operas I had missed by wasting time at school. School, for all its talk, has never really valued narrative the way it does "symbolism." My grandmother did not speak a word of English, but somehow could follow everything that happened on *As the World Turns*. It was the "coding" of serial narratives and its reliance on suspense and familiar outcomes, which lessened the need for complete literal comprehension.

By the time I became a teenager, I was impatient, frustrated, and tantalized by movies that were advertised as being rated "R." I knew these were movies that "went all the way," and showed sexy adult things that were forbidden to thirteen year olds. I grew up incredibly curious about everything around me and fascinated by what was not around (which was starting to seem like a lot). I also knew I was missing out on something growing up in what I started to feel was the middle of nowhere. I wanted to be in a big glamorous city, with cafés, restaurants, conversations about art and literature, and most of all "culture." My experiences so far had not amounted to much "culture" in comparison to the enormous amount of books and movies I had consumed. I had read Fitzgerald, Hemingway, Flaubert, and I wanted something more. I had also begun to despise myself, my skin color, and my people as not being capable of "true" experience and complexity.

Brownsville is a border town on the southernmost point of Texas and its population is about 95 percent Chicana/o. In his book, *Poorest of Americans: The Mexican-Americans of the Lower Rio Grande Valley of Texas*, Robert Lee Maril describes the Chicanos living there as being "among the poorest people in the United States. By every quantifiable measure which describes poverty, Valley Chicanos are much poorer than those who live in other cities and regions of this country" (4). By the time I was fifteen I figured out that I was not only racially and economically different from the "America" I had seen in movies, but sexually different too. My sense of sexual difference was also marked by the torch songs from the 1920s and 1930s by Gershwin, Porter, Rodgers and Hart, and Arlen that I was obsessed by. These had all informed my personality and had given me ideas about what romance should be: unhappy, emotional, and deep. Having seen quite a few movies by then, and also having discovered the aesthetic of melodramatic suffering so prevalent in Mexican Catholic culture, my ideas of love were quite intense.

It is interesting to me, too, the various books that I was required to read in high school. The texts that stand out sharply in my mind are: *Romeo and Juliet*, *A Streetcar Named Desire*, *Madame Bovary*, and *The Great Gatsby*. What stories of unrequited and repressed love! None of these is particularly optimistic about the possibilities of "true love," while they paradoxically entrust "love" with enormous significance and power. It was the most "American" of these texts, *The Great Gatsby*, which contains one of my favorite confrontations in literature. It occurs when Tom is finally confronted with Daisy and Gatsby's affair, which of course means much more to one than the other (someone loving more than the other is very dramatic and very Hollywood), Gatsby insists that Daisy admit she has never loved her husband, but she cannot: "Oh, you want too much! . . . I love you now—isn't that enough? I can't help what's past." It is true that Gatsby wants too much; he wants the past to match up to his own script of romantic fulfillment, and for the future to fulfill all his dreams of it. In other words, Gatsby wants life to be like a movie, where differences of any kind do not have to matter. He's like a film director intent on creating a world of his own design. His love for Daisy, and his fantasies about the future, however, ends unrequited—could anything have matched his dreams?

It was about this time that I met Jimmy de la Rosa, who was a year ahead of me in high school; we soon became inseparable. I was in love with him for so long, and we watched so many movies together, that I think of our relationship from *Blade Runner* to *Return of the Jedi*, to the movies we rented practically every night. We loved Woody Allen, especially *Annie Hall* and *Love and Death*. We would rent practically anything. Jimmy loved science fiction, I loved drama, but since I loved Jimmy, we watched a lot of sci-fi. We saw *A Clockwork Orange* but also *The Graduate*, *West Side Story*, and *Eraserhead*. We watched all of Monty Python (which I did not like) and anything that took place on some damn planet somewhere.

I remember once being at the movies with him watching some dumb thing just to pass the time. We were sitting next to each other, since thankfully, we did not submit to Chicano male etiquette which dictated that men sat with one empty seat between each other (someone told me he called it "the fag seat"). I remember sitting there wanting, yearning and stretching toward him, wanting to touch him, hold his hand. In the darkness, I could smell him, and I ached to make some type of physical contact with him, there in the flickering shadows, in the cool theater, scented with popcorn and carpet. Of course I didn't touch him, and I was struck years later, when I saw in William S. Burroughs' novel, *Queer*, his own experiences of lust in the cinema, while watching something a bit more highbrow: "Lee and Allerton went to see Cocteau's *Orpheus*. In the dark theater, Lee could feel his body pull towards Allerton, an amoeboid protoplasmic projection, straining with a blind worm hunger to enter the other's body, to breathe with his lungs, see with his eyes, learn the feel of his viscera and genitals. Allerton shifted in his seat. Lee felt a sharp twinge, a strain or dislocation of the spirit" (36). However much I strained, though, I never actually acted on my desire, and Jimmy remained physically remote from me. To paraphrase Marcel Proust, it was all in my head.

Our relationship was tortured, at least on my part. I knew how I felt about him, but it wasn't until I went away to school in Austin, Texas that

I began to feel more confident about my sexuality and my love for him. The university had film classes, art houses, and millions of books. I floundered around in my classes while I would watch at least three movies a day. This was fairly easy to do at the time. If a class was offered in "1930s Hollywood Comedies and Musicals," I would go to all their screenings (*Gold Diggers of 1933, A Night at the Opera, Top Hat, My Man Godfrey*). The university showed double features everyday, and that is where I fell in love with the melodramas of the great Bette Davis, like *All This and Heaven Too, The Great Lie, The Letter*, and of course, *All About Eve*. I also loved actresses like Jean Arthur (*The Devil and Miss Jones, The More the Merrier*), Rosalind Russell (*The Women, His Girl Friday*), and especially Barbara Stanwyck (*Baby Face, The Lady Eve*).

Of course, I fell in love with musicals. Judy Garland was my favorite, especially in *The Pirate* and *Meet Me in St. Louis. Kiss Me, Kate, Guys and Dolls*, and *Singin' in the Rain* were all big musicals of the 1950s that made a huge impression on me. It was also about this time that I discovered the psychodrama films made of Tennessee Williams' plays. I loved the emotional and theatrical atmosphere of *Summer and Smoke* and *Sweet Bird of Youth* but especially loved *A Streetcar Named Desire* and *Cat on a Hot Tin Roof*, with Elizabeth Taylor and Paul Newman. (Were two more beautiful people ever in a movie?) By this time, I knew I was gay. When I went home for the summer and told Jimmy that I had figured everything out, and that I was in love with him, things got a little tense. One afternoon, after a movie, *St. Elmo's Fire*, he told me firmly that he was straight and that we were good friends, but that was all. I had been writing him letters everyday from school, and had devoted many fantasies to our eventually—someday—getting together both sexually and emotionally. I was devastated, but it also started me thinking seriously about the poetics of unrequited love. Why would a gay man fall in love with a straight man—what was this romance of being attracted to the seemingly impossible? (Notice how the "seemingly" insinuated itself into the question.) But the fact of the matter was that I was drawn to these feelings of longing and poignancy. I drew a distinct pleasure from the idea of romantic suffering. Perhaps a romance with a straight man was a way of practically guaranteeing romantic failure, or maybe it was instead (or also) a refusal to accept the institutional realities of sexual orientation. And was this refusal tied into other refusals of authority?

As I began the formal process of coming out, I also began becoming politically active, and I joined MEChA, a Chicano activist organization, begun in the Chicano Movement, but still quite active on college campuses throughout the country. I started taking courses in Chicano, African-American, and Women's Studies. I began watching the cinema of political commitment like the great Soviet movies after the Revolution (*Mother*, *Earth*). I discovered French cinema, especially Godard (*Breathless*, *Weekend*) and Truffaut (*400 Blows*, *Jules et Jim*). I fell in love with Luis Buñel, too, especially his early movies like *Un Chien Andalou* and *L'Age d'Or*. One particular course definitively changed my thinking about movies and cultural production. It was on Italian cinema, and we saw the great movies of Fellini, Visconti, Bertolucci, and Pasolini, which all absolutely thrilled me. When I saw Vittoria de Sica's *Bicycle Thieves* the project of Italian neorealism seemed relevant to the entire problem of representation in the cinema—the film was a challenge to Hollywood conventions of narrative and glamour, and yet relied on Hollywood techniques of empathy and sentiment. The film was infused with a sharp sensibility of poignancy. The longing and sadness recalled the searching pain of unrequited love, yet this wasn't a romantic story. It was so much about the search for a stolen bicycle, at the same time it took on the search for justice, for fulfillment, in a world of inequities. The search for the bicycle is the search for "something better than this," the quest for a way out of such deprivation. This moment was crystallized when the bicycle is stolen from the father when he is pasting posters of the movie goddess Rita Hayworth onto walls. The father must recover his bicycle in order to maintain his livelihood. That he must depend on the mundane bicycle to feed his family—that the bicycle is necessary to spread Hollywood illusion throughout depressed post-war Rome—is one of the richest ironies of the film.

For me, film became part of my "real life" experiences—it shaped my sensibility of valuing the sensations of loss and melancholy, along with a longing to transform the painful into something meaningful and the junky into something valuable. This book is about these types of transformations and my sense that there is something utopian about believing in the possibility of transformation.

Chapter 1

The Boys in the Band: Camp and the Heartbreak of Race

In this chapter, I focus on Mart Crowley's play, *The Boys in the Band*, examining its use of mass cultural references and its diagetic investment in sentimentality. For the purposes of this discussion, I describe these expressive discourses as "camp." My organizing concerns are defining, at least provisionally, what camp is and how it is historically and socially formed and circulated. I also consider the question of gay male racial formation and suggest that within the parameters of the play, camp cannot fully account for racial difference except through degradation and humiliation. Since the play is heavily invested in "camping," as central to gay humor, especially in its references to race, I begin with this point.

Camp can be understood as a version of gay male in-joking, and therefore can also operate as exclusionary, in distinct ways. First, since camp relies on a certain amount of irreverence, it can often utilize racist and sexist stereotypes to achieve these effects. Race and gender can become sites of gay male camp—not all of it politically progressive, and not all of it especially funny to those who are its targets. This inevitable alliance of camp with insult, and even with humiliation, is a central focus of Mart Crowley's dynamics. Second, camp is also about textual references, a cultural name-dropping that often relies on class and educational privileges. This referencing, by its design, depends on its own version of history and value and creates its own sentimental nostalgia. In fact, it is ironic that for all of camp's reputation for subverting high and mass culture, it often creates its own hierarchical investments. This particular limitation of camp involves its own decisiveness on what constitutes "gay culture" itself—an important dynamic indeed in identity formation, particularly for those routinely excluded from its scope. Third, the relationship of camp to the formation of a politicized gay male identity is a troubling and far from settled one. It has been argued that camp is central to a "gay male sensibility," and it is even seen by some as a reactionary manifestation of this "sensibility." Camp can be read by some gays and lesbians as a relic of a self-hating era or by others as testimony to the inventive inversion of mass cultural codes by gays and lesbians. But because camp relies so intensely upon extreme and dramatic trivialization or exaggeration, it can too readily dismiss what it finds too serious or solemn. This limitation of camp involves its peculiar relationship to "politics," to the public sphere, and its difficulty in forging tools of meaningful political struggle. I include Crowley's play in this discussion, although unlike many of the other works in this book, it is not composed by a person of color, yet it highlights issues pertinent to how white gay culture represents questions of race. I am also drawn to the play's representation of the experience of unrequited love.

The Play

The Boys in the Band opened in 1968, one year prior to the Stonewall Rebellion in New York City, but the movie version appeared in 1970, one year after Stonewall. In brief, Stonewall is generally considered the beginning of the Gay Liberation Movement. On the weekend of June 19, 1969, after a police raid of the Stonewall Inn in New York City, its patrons, consisting mainly of drag queens and people of color, fought back and refused to surrender their ground. What began as a bar fight on a hot summer night in fact became a vitally important part of the 1960s and early 1970s struggle for social justice. This locates the play in an interesting position: representing the vibrancy of gay culture prior to Stonewall and remaining a representation of gay life from which post-Stonewall gays may have come to radically distance themselves. For my purposes, since the play in no overt way begins to "politicize" its subject, it offers a productive and historical perspective on the entanglements of sexuality and race, as they concern camp and the formation of gay male identity.

The Boys in the Band takes its title from a seminal Judy Garland/Warner Brothers movie from 1954, *A Star is Born*. One of the highlights of the film is when James Mason discovers an unknown Judy Garland after hours at a nightclub, singing with her backup band. As Mason watches unobserved, Garland sings Harold Arlen and Ira Gershwin's "The Man that Got Away." Later in the film, James Mason reassures Garland, who, though her talent and his patronage have made her famous and successful, is nervous to sing before an audience, "Relax, it's three a.m. at the Downbeat Club, and you're singing for yourself and the boys in the band." Mart Crowley's title instantly signifies the play's all male cast (with a campy hint of a musical), along with a trivia reference that would not be readily apparent to all of its audiences, gay or straight. *The Boys in the Band* opened onstage on April 15, 1968 at the Theater Four, off-Broadway in New York City. It was directed by Robert Moore and was a smash hit, running for over 1,000 performances. The distinguished theater critic, Harold Clurman, reviewed the play in May 1968 for *New York* magazine, and described it as "skillful and amusing in its dialogue . . . brilliantly cast, very well acted and admirably directed." Clurman notices the centrality of camp to the play, but inflects the production with a serious purpose: "Though full of camp fun, *The Boys in the Band* is not a cheap exploitation of its subject. It aims to show the guilt and self-loathing (often masquerading as impertinence and brash self-advertisement) from which many homosexuals, like members of all minorities, suffer" (695). In *The New York Times*, drama critic Clive Barnes called it "by far the frankest treatment of homosexuality I have ever seen." Barnes did have reservations about the "relentlessness" of the camp humor, but acknowledged how pervasive this urban sensibility had become: "The New York wit, famous the world over, is little more than a mixture of Jewish humor and homosexual humor seen through the bottom of a dry martini glass" (Kaiser 187–188).

But gay critic Michael Bronski, in his book *Culture Clash: The Making of the Gay Sensibility* describes the play quite differently: "Crowley's characters camped their way through more than two of hours of creaking melodrama. Playwright Crowley made sure the heterosexual critics and audiences saw what they really believed: gay men who were unhappy and willfully cruel to one another." He does note that "whatever its pandering to homophobia, *The Boys in the Band* created possibilities for presenting gay material on the screen" (131). Importantly, Bronski's reaction has become the standard gay critical response to this work. The play has been variously described as dated, stereotypical, and filled with self-loathing, but given credit for opening up gay camp as a public representation of gay male culture.

Indeed, the play was successful enough to become a major Hollywood studio movie in 1970, directed by William Friedkin. It is this movie version that insured the play's dissemination into gay popular culture. Vito Russo, in his important book, *The Celluloid Closet: Homosexuality in the Movies*, points out that the "film was a special project in Hollywood and it was handled with a fidelity to the text that was more appropriate to a *Long Day's Journey into Night*" (174). While Russo's book is a serious and thorough examination of homophobic stereotypes in Hollywood movies since the silent era, it is also in some ways a dialogue with other film critics, including and especially, *The New Yorker* film critic, Pauline Kael and her sometimes homophobic, yet acerbic remarks. Kael, in a particularly caustic (but funny) review in 1970, describes the play as:

> Actors carrying-on on-stage as actors often do backstage, and it's a theater piece that has lost its theatrically satisfying form, and what was bad is now worse, while what was passable because it "played well" doesn't play so well on the screen. Maybe because the author, Mart Crowley, is the producer, the text has been preserved as if the quips were ageless and pure gold (and they're delivered with knee-whacking emphasis), and the director brings out the worst of the play with guilt-ridden pauses and long see-the-suffering-in-the-face close-ups. Every blink and lick of the lips has its rigidly scheduled meaning, and it's all so solemn—like Joan Crawford when she's thinking. The actors sweat so freely that the movie seems to have moved the party to the baths. (274)

It is interesting to note that both Russo and Kael use a version of campy, bitchy humor to decry what they see as an inflated sense of importance towards the play's material. Russo contrasts Crowley's play with the height of U.S. dramaturgy, Eugene O'Neill's epic masterpiece of familial disintegration through drugs and illusion, while Kael references two venerable gay institutions, Joan Crawford and the baths. If Joan Crawford has now become the representation in gay camp humor of the devouring, driven mother shrieking about wire hangers, in Kael's 1970 context, she was more of an unreal, Old Hollywood campy relic, and relatively less of a monster. (In fact, even in the 1962 *Whatever Happened to Baby Jane?* Crawford played the sympathetic role to Bette Davis' harridan.) Kael sees *The Boys in the Band* as invested in camp humor that has grown stale, that takes itself too seriously, and that has become cliché. Her sarcasm about Crawford's tedious thinking removes her image from the world of the intellect, and places her in a celluloid void. Yet, she makes this criticism while partaking and indulging in the very terms of that humor. To talk about camp, it seems, always involves the risk and the pleasure of being campy. Or conversely, by strictly avoiding the lure of campy humor, the analysis risks its own ridiculousness, relying on an unironic sobriety to make its sober point.

The Uses of Camp

Gay male camp, especially that involving movies, musical theater, and other types of performance, seems to provoke responses that recognize the silliness and the absurd pathos of that intense investment. *The Boys in the Band*, which has come to represent a virtual catalog of these campy stereotypes, is itself aware of this effect. For example, at the beginning of the play, Michael, the lead character, tries to cheer up his friend, Donald, by singing one of Judy Garland's most famous songs, "Get Happy." The stage directions read: "Michael does a few Garland poses. Sees Donald isn't buying it." Michael then asks, "What's more boring than a queen doing a Judy Garland imitation?" Donald replies, "A queen doing a Bette Davis imitation." Here, the "boringness," the predictability, of camp icons is resisted, even reviled—at the same time that it is partaken in. Garland and Davis, then, are enshrined into the play's own version of gay iconography.

This discussion specifically looks at how the play dramatizes various definitions of camp in order to investigate the potency of camp humor, potency perhaps caused by the contradictions upon which it operates. If camp is notoriously difficult to define, to begin to understand it in the context of dramatic theater, and in a particular historical context, may make the task less formidable. But defining camp and homophobic responses to it should not deflect from making criticisms of camp's limitations, and its tendencies toward degradation and impotent bitterness.

The Cast of Characters

The Boys in the Band has a cast of nine men, eight of them (fairly) out as gay men. They have all gathered in a "smartly appointed duplex apartment in the East Fifties, New York," to celebrate Harold's birthday. It is Michael's apartment, and he is the center of the play, setting its events in motion and acting as a spokesperson for gay male self-hatred and self-destruction. Vito Russo quotes Crowley describing his character, Michael: "Nobody would try to pass Michael off as having today's consciousness . . . All the negative things in the play are represented by Michael, and because he's the leading character it was his message that a very square American public wanted to receive" (177). Michael is indeed the most unpleasant character in the play, and the play's reputation of sodden bitterness mostly stems from him. Through the course of the narrative, he becomes very drunk and proceeds to assault each of his guests for their various failings.

Emory is the "queen" of the group and plays the most with camp humor, often targeting Bernard, who is described in the dramatis personae as "twenty-eight, Negro, nice looking." Donald seems to be Michael's best friend, and is described by Larry as "a very serious reader, having gone through all of Doris Lessing's novels in a week because he was depressed." Larry and Hank are a long-standing couple and are both described as good looking and athletic; they also are the "straightest" acting of the bunch. Harold, the birthday boy, is described as "thirty-two, dark, lean, strong limbs, unusual Semitic face," and his "birthday gift" (from Emory) is Cowboy, a comely male hustler, who Michael mocks mercilessly for being his intellectual inferior. Finally, there is Alan, Michael's "straight" college roommate from Georgetown who is having problems in his marriage and unexpectedly (and disastrously) drops by the party.

Despite the fact that the party is at Michael's apartment, he does everything he can to make everyone feel unwelcome and miserable. Yet, in a typical device used in haunted house horror movies, nobody can just get up and leave. Michael describes his dread of the evening to Donald before anyone has even arrived: "If there's one thing I'm not ready for, it's five screaming queens singing happy birthday... I think you know everybody anyway—they're the same old tired fairies you've seen around since the day one" (7–8). Further, in the opening scene, both Michael and Donald describe their general unhappiness over their wretched lives. Donald is early because his therapist canceled and makes a long speech (clearly intended for the therapist) about realizing how he's "never finished anything in my life," and how he began to "identify failing with winning my mother's love. And I began to fail on purpose to get it. I didn't finish Cornell... Failure is the only thing with which I feel at home. Because it is what I was taught at home" (10). Donald's self-analysis, which combines, in vaguely stereotypical Freudian terms, homosexuality with a type of Oedipal failure, is taken up by Michael—although he uses another popular Freudian explanation for homosexuality, "immaturity."

Michael makes his self-mocking speech in the antic, if not obnoxious, spirit of camp references: "I'm a spoiled brat so what do I know about being mature. The only thing mature means to me is Victor Mature who was in all those pictures with Betty Grable. (Sings a la Grable) 'I can't begin to tell you how much you mean to me...' Betty sang that in 1945... '45?—'43. No, '43 was *Coney Island* which was remade in '50 as *Wabash Avenue*. Yes, *Dolly Sisters* was in '45" (11). Donald trivializes Michael's enthusiasm, as well as his campy knowledge of movie trivia: "How did I manage to miss these momentous events in the American Cinema? I can understand people having an affinity for stage—but movies are such garbage, who can take them seriously?" Michael replies to Donald's snobbery, with an acute awareness of cultural privilege, "Well, I'm sorry if your sense of art is offended. Odd as it may seem there was no Schubert Theater in Hot Coffee, Mississippi!" Donald then recognizes what this sense of movie camp has bothered Michael: "However, thanks to the silver screen, your neurosis has got style" (11–12). If Michael's neurosis has "style," the question is raised in the framework of their conversation whether or not his investment in movies comes from his homosexuality, or if the two are unrelated. The pathologizing of camp discourse, or at least the trivialization of its knowledge may come from a recognition of it being part of the stigmatization of being gay. To insist on being "campy" is in some way to be neurotic, unhealthy, and queer. Here camp is brought into a discourse of aesthetic investments and cultural values, and Michael is accused of not being able to distinguish and identify what is important and what is art. (Theater is "Art." Movies are "garbage.") To be camp is to reject the normative, institutional definition of "important art." Camp also, then, rejects "rational" responses to emotional distress and in some way, causes "neurosis." It is an inability to "maturely" distinguish between the trivial and the important. In camp's scheme, aesthetic values of bad and good are almost, if not entirely, beside the point. In fact an overvaluing of what is aesthetically "bad" or inappropriately grandiose can perhaps begin to define camp's essence.

The campiest character (by design) in the play is Emory, who is thirty-three (the oldest of the bunch), and who is described as "small, frail, very plain." Emory provides the most laughs in the text, and unfortunately receives the most brutal treatment, especially from Alan, Michael's straight ex-roommate. When Michael learns that Alan might drop by the party, he immediately instructs everyone, "Now please everybody, do me a favor and cool it for the few minutes he's here." Emory replies, "Anything for a sis, Mary." Michael is enraged: "That's exactly what I'm talking about, Emory. No camping!" Emory responds: "Sorry. (Sits left end. Deep, deep voice to Donald.) Think the Giants are gonna win the pennant this year?" Emory's response to being told not to camp, and to act like a man, is, in fact, to campily "act like a man." He relies on a signifier of "straight" maleness, quoting the Giants as a masculine stereotype, which pointedly excludes him. This may also account for negative responses to camp since camp is never, never "masculine."

Camp and Masculinity

For a man to act campily is to at least momentarily forsake his investment in male privilege. In acting campily, gay men may refer to each other as "sis" or "girl" or any other feminine terminology. This feminizing power of camp is important not only in its possible effects—hostility, shame—but also, in its formation of a gay male subject. This "femininity" obviously does not rely on biological gender, but also does not necessarily rely on socially gendered expectations either. Often to camp is not to act like a "woman" and is often not to act like any socially recognizable man *or* woman. It is to feminize manhood, to make a mockery of the unselfconsciousness of maleness, to put maleness in quotes—"manhood." Camp language then becomes a defining and organizing part of a gay male identity. This campy vernacular ensures that the "feminine" will be vital to what it means to be "gay." But the question remains about exactly why the feminine has anything to do with gay male identity at all. This gender linkage has become almost completely unremarked upon both in and out of gay culture, but in the course of the play, the feminine and feminine-coded language provokes various acts of violence, which link a hatred of the feminine with homophobia. But on more general terms, the play itself functions to "naturalize" the connection between femininity and gay male identity.

What linguist and anthropologist, William L. Leap refers to as "Gay Men's English" is in fact heavily indebted to definitions of camp. Leap in his book (1994) explicitly discusses the effect that *The Boys in the Band* had on him:

> The first time I really listened to Gay English was in Albuquerque, New Mexico, in 1969. I was sitting in a movie theater watching the film version of Mart Crowley's play ... I had already learned a few things about the folklore surrounding gay speech from high school locker-room conversations and joke telling, late night college dormitory conversations, and my few gay encounters while in graduate school. But before I saw this film, I had not been party to any type of sustained conversation (however artificially constructed) between gay men. I was enchanted by the scenario displayed in that narrative—chic rooftop apartments in Manhattan, summers on Fire Island, a close circle of gay friends, meeting regularly for cocktails and clever conversation. I was also struck both by the creativeness of these men's verbal exchange and by the viciousness that colored its tone. (12)

Camp, then, is also about skill, about being able to quickly and wittily come up with responses and defenses. Camping is also a way of resisting normativity and a means of fighting back strategically and cleverly with language. So, while camp functions as a feature of stigmatization by its association with femininity, it can also operate as a weapon of defiance. In the play, these features are painfully dramatized.

An example of this hatred of the feminine occurs when the straight character, Alan, enters the party while everyone but Hank is dancing to Martha and the Vendellas' "Heat Wave." His entrance unfortunately interrupts one of the few moments when the "boys" actually seem to be having fun. Alan's straight presence causes everyone to become self-conscious, and Michael lamely makes excuses on everyone's behalf. When Alan is introduced one by one to Michael's friends, he is also introduced to Emory's incessantly campy language. For example, Alan asks where Harold is after he is told it is his birthday that is being celebrated, and Emory explains his absence, "She's never been on time." The stage directions then read: "Bernard nudges Emory with his knee. Michael shoots Emory a withering glance." If camp is feminizing, it can also operate as a community cultural code. In society at large, here represented by Alan, it is clearly inappropriate (if not immoral) to refer to men as "she." (As we shall see a little later, sometimes it is not only inappropriate, it can be physically dangerous.)

If Alan (and by default everyone else) is embarrassed by Emory's behavior and talk, he is very much taken by Hank, Larry's straight-acting partner:

ALAN: I'm a lawyer. What . . . do you do?
HANK: I teach school.
ALAN: Oh. I would have taken you for an athlete of some sort.
You look as if you might play sports.
HANK: Well, I'm not professional but I was on the basketball team in college and I play quite of bit of tennis.
ALAN: I play tennis too.
HANK: Great game.
ALAN: Yes. Great. (A beat. Silence as LARRY, BERNARD, AND EMORY look bored.) What . . . do you teach?
HANK: Math.
ALAN: Math?
HANK: Yes.
ALAN: Math. Well. (34)

This "suggestive" conversation is finally interrupted by Emory who decodes its nuances immediately by cracking, "Kinda makes you want to rush out and buy a slide rule, doesn't it?" Emory's crude remark is blatantly sexual at the same time that his interruption disrupts a subtly yet sexually tense exchange. Camp has interrupted the solemnity of "man talk," along with sexualizing publicly an admittedly banal exchange. Hank and Alan, in fact, are having the stereotypically male conversation that Emory mocked earlier, but with an erotically submerged conversational rhythm. Emory is too campy to participate in this decidedly male exchange, but he uses camp to point out what it may really be about. Indeed, the conversation is also virtually staccato, marked by pauses and short words. Crowley even notes the extra beat where it should occur, signaling that this conversation is the type that two people engage in who are attracted to each other, and who are intrigued even by mundane information about each other. Even silences in this type of conversation function to generate an uncomfortable, yet potent erotic energy. In dramatic terms, a "beat" signals a moment that has gone on a bit too long, that has stretched up to a point of discomfort or heightened expression. A conversation can be filled with beats, especially when sexual tension has made verbal expression impossible. Perhaps if Emory had not interrupted, Alan and Hank would have continued to say "Math" to each other infinitely, or perhaps the tension would have been stretched to the breaking point. It is also notable that Emory's remark points out the symbolic masculinity of Hank's teaching of math. If Hank had said he taught poetry or drama, the sexual effect would have been differently inflected, if perhaps made more difficult to discern.

In this exchange, another characteristic of camp is foregrounded—campiness is generally not found sexually attractive or compelling by gay men. Alan and Hank are attracted to each other—despite their ostensibly different sexual orientations—because they are both "normal," masculine, and because they don't camp. Their conversation continues:

ALAN: You're married?
HANK: What?
ALAN: I see you're married. (He points to Hank's wedding band.)
HANK: Oh.
MICHAEL: Yes. Hank's married.
ALAN: You have any kids?
HANK: Yes. Two. A boy nine, and a girl seven. You should see my boy play tennis—really puts his dad to shame.
ALAN: I have two kids too. Both girls.
HANK: Great. (35)

I quote these passages because in a play that is characterized and criticized for its outrageous and expressive campiness, these stand out as the dullest exchanges. Crowley is parodying what a heterosexual exchange "sounds like" to gay people. He also is foregrounding how heterosexuality proclaims itself as incessantly and tediously as homosexuality is often accused of doing. Hank and Alan's conversation is filled with markers of "heterosexuality," and these markers are about the most conventional details. This is the kind of talk that Alan feels comfortable with, and what he would consider "decent" conversation. What he cannot abide is Emory's incessant flaunting of these conventions. Emory can't even simply say that someone is always late, but must theatricalize and feminize it as, "She is always late."

If Alan is disturbed by Michael's party, it is Emory he scapegoats as the unacceptable "Other." When he and Michael retreat from the party, he tells him:

> ALAN: Your friends all seem like very nice guys. That Hank is really a very attractive fellow.
> MICHAEL: ... Yes. He is.
> ALAN: We have a lot in common ... I like Donald too. The only one I didn't care too much for was—what's his name—Emory?
> MICHAEL: Yes. Emory.
> ALAN: I just can't stand that kind of talk. It just grates on me.
> MICHAEL: What kind of talk, Alan?
> ALAN: Oh, you know. His brand of humor, I guess.
> MICHAEL: He can be really quite funny sometimes.
> ALAN: I suppose so. If you find that sort of thing amusing. He just seems like such a goddamn little pansy. (Silence. A pause. He steps away.) I'm sorry I said that. I didn't mean to say that ... but you have to admit he is effeminate ... He's like a butterfly in heat! I couldn't care less what people do—as long as they don't do it in public—or—or try to force their ways on the whole damned world. (39–40)

Alan's reaction to Emory is not unlike many men, both gay and straight, who see effeminate gay men as deeply embarrassing, with gay men often holding them responsible for the existence of public homophobia itself. Effeminacy is perceived as deliberately provoking violence, for which straight men cannot be held accountable. Alan certainly is willing to be tolerant—up to a point. But what needs to be stressed is that the thing that Alan hates the most about Emory is his manner of speaking, which becomes Emory's entire, abject identity. In this sense, speech becomes not only camp, but also another marker of gay identity itself.

Homosexual Panic

Alan's definitive response to Emory's talk is to physically attack him. After his talk with Michael, he is preparing to leave the party, and he tells Hank that when he is in Washington, he would like him to meet his wife. Larry, his lover, makes a sarcastic remark about it, and Emory cuts in, once again, reading the situation for what it "really" is:

> EMORY: Yeah, they'd love to meet him—her. I have such a problem with pronouns.
> ALAN: (Quick, to Emory): How many esses are there in the word pronoun?
> EMORY: How'd you like to kiss my ass—that's got two or more essessss in it!
> ALAN: How'd you like to blow me!
> EMORY: What's the matter with your wife, she got lockjaw?
> ALAN: (Lashes out) Faggot, Fairy, pansy . . . (Lunges at Emory, grabs him, pulls him off stool to floor and attacks him fiercely.) queer cocksucker! I'll kill you, you goddamn little mincing swish! You goddamn freak! FREAK! FREAK! (Pandemonium! EVERYONE overlaps words. ALAN has quickly beaten EMORY to the floor before anyone has recovered from the surprise, and reacted to move.) (45)

Alan is pulled off of Emory, right in time for Harold's arrival, whose laugh at the entire scene ends the first act of the play. The pandemonium Alan causes sets in motion a series of various recriminations. It could be argued that Alan's outburst is a type of homosexual panic—he realizes his own homosexual feelings toward Hank, and attacks Emory in retaliation. What I would like to emphasize is that Alan in fact causes part of the ugliness associated with the play, an ugliness that is often attributed to the gay men's own self-loathing and unhappiness. Alan is a force that violently crashes upon the characters with his uninvited presence provoking feelings of shame and humiliation. That he chooses to lash out at Emory once again reinforces Emory's marginality and vulnerability even within his own gay world. Meanwhile, Emory stands the least chance of "passing" in Alan's straight world, since his behavior and his language indelibly mark him with the stigma of the unvalued, the despised, and the most pathetic.

Camp and Race

But if Emory is clearly the most "oppressed" of the group, and the subject of the physical abuse, it is interesting that his friendship with Bernard seems predicated on some type of shared bond. (Bernard being the only person of color in the cast.) Emory and Bernard are thrown together in the dynamics of the play, and their specific positions create a unique relationship between them. Despite himself being marginalized by the group, Emory is quick to make campy racist remarks regarding Bernard. Some of the racist remarks that Emory makes about Bernard include:

- Emory, upon Bernard's entrance, cries out, "It's the queen of spades!"
- In a reply to an insult from Bernard, "Why don't you have a piece of watermelon and hush up!"
- Music is turned on and when Bernard responds enthusiastically, Emory says, "A drum beat and their eyes sparkle like Cartier's."
- After Michael orders Emory to the kitchen, Bernard tells him that he is a "natural born domestic." Emory replies, "Said the African queen! You come on too—you can fan me while I make the salad dressing."
- Emory asks Bernard where the wineglasses are:

    BERNARD: Ahz workin as fas' as ah can! (A la Butterfly McQueen.)
    EMORY: They have to be told everything. Can't let 'em out of your sight.

Emory's jokes, which are clearly offensive, are supposed to be taken in the context of the play's general sense of gay bar humor and campiness. The threshold for racist humor in this type of articulation of gay male camp is quite high. It can be argued that the "underground" aspect of any white subculture seems to suspend liberal bourgeois pretenses of racial politeness. Since Emory is estranged from the larger "mainstream" culture, different standards of politeness can apply, and make this type of joking more acceptable. But sometimes the ground on which much of camp rests—that of irreverence, and disdain for the morally and politically serious—can have racist effects. This suspension of any moral authority makes it difficult to counter this "humor" without sounding self-righteous and grim (or that you haven't gotten the joke). It is also difficult to launch any type of sustained critique, although these types of jokes would seem to require instant, uncomplicated condemnation. But I want to analyze how Emory's remarks are interpreted within the terms of the play. In the second act of the play, everything becomes much more serious, and every campy remark, racist or otherwise, becomes quite sinister and grave.

Affairs of the Heart

As Harold puts it, "the revolution is complete" when Michael announces that no one can leave what is becoming an increasingly unfun party until they play a game. He describes the game as being a version of "Murder" and "The Truth Game" ("They're quite similar. The rules are the same in both—you kill somebody," Donald remarks.) that he calls "Affairs of the Heart." The game involves earning a number of points for telephoning someone who they have truly loved and telling the person, "I love you." It is this party game that supplies what is most notorious about the play's politics and also that gives the play its derivative, mechanical structure. The emotional breakdowns that result come directly from a somewhat clumsy device, a game that is finally supposed to reveal the "truth" of its players. What was once campy and fun now becomes embittered and pathetic.

The derivativeness of Crowley's aesthetic project is clear in its imitation of Edward Albee's 1962 play, *Who's Afraid of Virginia Woolf?* Interestingly (or maybe, in a slight tip of his hand), just prior to the game, Michael announces to everyone eating that, "Ladies and ladies, I would like to announce that you have just eaten Sebastian Veneble." This is a reference to Tennessee Williams' *Suddenly, Last Summer*, and this is discussed between the characters:

HANK: Did Edward Albee write that play?
MICHAEL: No. Tennessee Williams.
HANK: Oh, yeah.
MICHAEL: Albee wrote *Who's Afraid of Virginia Woolf?*
LARRY: Dummy.
COWBOY: Edward who?
MICHAEL: How much did you pay for him?

This deliberate referencing of Williams and Albee aims to link Crowley's play not only with the work of the two greatest American playwrights at the time (along with Arthur Miller, of course), but with the specific gay context of their work (excepting Arthur Miller, of course).

The Great American Gay Theater

The references to Williams and Albee indeed point toward two of the most famous playwrights of the post-war era, and both influenced Crowley's "gay" aesthetic. Both have been reclaimed as *gay* writers, although they emerged from different creative contexts and each of their relationships to homosexuality in their lives and art operate differently.

In the 1960s, their plays were subject to controversy when drama critics began expressing their uneasiness and hostility toward a perceived overwhelming homosexual influence in the American theater. Michael Bronski quotes a critic in 1967 who wrote an article attacking Albee entitled, "Who's Afraid of Little Annie Fanny":

> The point is that homosexual playwrights and homosexual directors and homosexual producers are having more and more to say about what can and can't be done in the American theater . . . I'm getting damned tired of all art being campy and all the plays being queer and all the clothes being West Fourth Street and the whole bit. Some I don't mind, but it's getting too close to all, and I have the feeling that there are healthier bases for culture. (125)

Critics were not only alarmed that many of the leading playwrights were gay, but they were also concerned that theater itself, and the forms they were accustomed to, were being unforgivably altered into perversion. The concern for "healthier bases" belies the anxiety that theater was being contaminated by perverse influences. Playwrights like Albee at this time were experimenting with theatrical structure, along with holding an unsympathetic lens to American institutions such as consumerism and the nuclear family. One-act plays such as *The Sandbox* (1960) and *The American Dream* (1961) were American absurdist satires on the banality and emptiness of life in the United States. Williams, less of a satirist but a social critic nonetheless, had long been accused of masquerading his gay male characters as neurotic, unrealistic women, groping for impossible love.

Camp was an affront to the unironic stance that many critics held towards what they saw as basic American values which needed to be strengthened by cultural representations, not campily eroded. That camp was a homosexual phenomenon solidified their suspicions that, like communists, "homosexuals were everywhere and they were destroying the world's natural, moral order" (Bronski 125). Stanley Kaufman, drama critic for *The New York Times* throughout the 1960s, responded to the controversy with his belief that gay playwrights who:

> . . . presented a badly distorted picture of American women, marriage, and society in general . . . their plays were streaked with vindictiveness towards the society that . . . discriminates against them. Camp can be seen, I believe, as an instrument of revenge on the main body of society. Theme and subject are important historical principles in our art. The arguments to prove that they are of diminishing importance—in fact, ought never to have been important—are cover for an attack on the idea

of social relevance. By adulation of sheer style, this group tends to deride the whole culture and the society that produced it, tends to reduce art to a clever game which even society cannot keep from playing. (126)

Kaufman's concern about the "adulation of sheer style" critically makes a distinction between, for example, "historical principles" and the sheer triviality of camp history. Again, too, there is the concern that homosexual men are incapable of "truly" representing what women are like.

Another commentator, William Goldman, who as a novelist, playwright, critic, and screenwriter, had already spent much time in show business, wrote a book about contemporary Broadway in 1967–1968, entitled *The Season: A Candid Look at Broadway*. In a chapter entitled, "Homosexuals," he attempts to calculate just exactly how many homosexuals are involved in the New York theater:

> Of the 58 productions listed in *Variety's* year-end survey as either "successes," "failures," "status not yet determined" or "closed during tryout or preview," at least 18, or 31%, were produced by homosexuals. Of the same 58 productions, at least 22, or 38%, were directed by homosexuals . . . As I said these figures are low. I think it would be safe to estimate that in any given Broadway season, anywhere from a third to a half of the producer-director talent is homosexual . . . the most famous playwrights tend to be associated with homosexuality. (237)

Goldman's concern is that the creative homosexual is forced to "dissemble," meaning that he writes "boy–girl relationships when he really means boy–boy relationships." This leads to the phenomenon on Broadway that the leading experts on heterosexual married life are "bachelors." Goldman wonders "if their knowledge of and attitude towards the subject might not be a little limited." The chapter culminates with Goldman expressing that he thinks "one of the most important events of the Broadway season was the blockbuster success off-Broadway of Mart Crowley's terrific homosexual play, 'The Boys in the Band.' It would be marvelous if this success started Broadway toward a sexual freedom it has never attained. After all, the homosexual is here, and he's not going anywhere. It might be nice to know, at last, what's really on his mind" (240). Goldman is willing to concede the homosexual playwright his importance on the dramatic scene, but still seems unwilling to formalize his presence in the formation of the contemporary drama.

The resentment and mixed admiration that these critics are experiencing also comes out of an intellectual milieu in which Susan Sontag's

"Notes on Camp" had made quite an impression. Therefore, let us briefly discuss this pioneering essay.

Sontag and Camp

Published in *The Partisan Review* in 1964, Sontag's essay made a case for what she characterized as "Camp." Sontag's alertness toward sensibilities, and her position of being (as the title of her collection of essays suggests) *Against Interpretation*, drew her quite naturally to the discourse of camp. Historicizing Sontag's project, Andrew Ross sees how the "importance of her own critical intervention in the mid-1960s was in the service of pleasure and erotics, and against judgment, truth, seriousness, and interpretation; against in short, the hermeneutics of depth and discrimination through which the New York intellectuals had filtered extra-curricular literary taste since the war" (147). Camp in this way provided a precise form in which to lodge a position that could escape plain moral sobriety. In camp, the aesthetic reveled in sheer excess, and one could both appreciate intense beauty and be ironic about its true use-value.

"Notes on Camp" consists of various thoughts about camp's aims as well as numbered "fragments" that attempt to provide examples of camp. Sontag begins by noting that: "A sensibility is one of the hardest things to talk about . . . the essence of camp is its love of the unnatural: of artifice and exaggeration . . . camp is esoteric—something of a private code, a badge of identity among small urban cliques . . . to talk about camp is therefore to betray it" (276). Sontag defends her ability to analyze something so ephemeral by declaring, in what was (and still is) one of her more controversial pronouncements:

> I am strongly drawn to Camp, and almost as strongly offended by it. That is why I want to talk about it, and why I can. For no one who wholeheartedly shares in a given sensibility can analyze it; he can only, whatever his intention, exhibit it. To name a sensibility, to draw its contours and to recount its history, requires a deep sympathy modified by revulsion. (276)

The words that Sontag uses in this introduction to her essay are infused with a certain gay context, especially in a framework in which 1950s mores were being increasingly challenged: "unnatural," "artifice," "exaggeration," and "esoteric" can refer to a gay urban enclave estranged from "mainstream" values and which exists in opposition to the "natural" conventional, middle-class, suburban family.

Other terms like "private code," "badge of identity," "small urban clique," along with the threat of "betrayal," circulate in a narrative in which identities and communities remain obscured. This seems to suggest what is referred to in contemporary terms as the Closet: the space of both imposed and preferred privacy and secrecy, a type of hermetic withdrawal from how the world goes about its "serious" public business. In a sense, Sontag was "outing" camp in 1964, and declaring it to be a gay sensibility. However, she seems to stop just short of this at the very end of the essay: "While it's not true that camp taste is homosexual taste, there is no doubt a peculiar affinity and overlap . . . so not all homosexuals have camp taste. But homosexuals, by and large, constitute the vanguard—and the most articulate audience of camp" (290). This seems to want to have it both ways since while it is true that not all "homosexuals" use, know, or care about camp in any of its many articulations, it is fair to say that camp is a particular homosexual creation (that nonhomosexuals can partake in). It is problematic (and often politically unwise) to assign identities to cultural activities, but in this instance, the context is fraught not only with the potential of homophobia to eradicate and erase "gayness," but also the danger of essentializing a gay identity as being solely constituted around camp.

Esther Newton, an anthropologist, in her important work on drag queens during the mid-1960s, *Mother Camp: Female Impersonators in America*, describes an interview she had with a "college educated" drag queen. Newton had given her a copy of Sontag's essay to read and describes how the drag queen was "enraged (justifiably, I felt) that she had almost edited homosexuals out of camp" (106). What is being expressed here is that camp is gay and any manifestation or analysis that does not recognize this is historically missing the point and rendering a group of people culturally invisible. This reading sees Sontag pulling gayness out of camp—at the same time that this gayness is recognized, it is not given thematic primacy in interpreting camp's cultural effects. Sontag's essay, granted, is situated several years before Stonewall's politicizing reach, but there is a rhetorical aggression in determining fully what the parameters of any cultural expression should be. In the context of Sontag's essay, it is close to impossible to consider why and how camp is a means of gay expression, or why it uses the modes of expression it does, and whether these modes are subject to change, or what historical contexts have affected the dynamics of camp as a cultural formation.

Furthermore, Sontag uses problematic language to describe her own intense, yet fractured relationship to camp. She claims she is as "strongly drawn" as she is "offended" by it. This, she argues (in, I think, a somewhat peculiar way) qualifies her to neutrally describe camp most effectively, since her revulsion toward what she is describing keeps her from becoming implicated, and thereby possibly offering a distorted view of it. In this sense Sontag seems to be declaring her distance from homosexuality in general, and perhaps offering a way of being able to talk about it without actually talking about it.

Sontag is correct, however, that camp is a notoriously difficult concept to define in any definite way. As is typical in these sorts of discussions, a list is offered of examples of what camp might be:

Zuleika Dobson
Tiffany lamps
Scoptione films
The Brown Derby restaurant on Sunset Boulevard in LA
The Enquirer, headlines and stories
Aubrey Beardsley drawings
"Swan Lake"
Bellini's operas . . . (107)

Sontag explains how entire art forms have become "saturated with camp. Classical ballet, opera, movies have seemed so for a long time" (107). She claims Art Nouveau is the "best example . . . the most typical and fully developed Camp style" (108). Art Nouveau's decorative emphasis and its metamorphic qualities, in which objects and shapes function as doorways or frames are indeed a type of camp ideal, but it also maintains camp as existing out of any engagement with the social formation.

Sontag is also in tune with camp's expressive function, which she describes as coming out:

> Most clearly in the vulgar use of the word camp as a verb, "to camp," something that people do. To camp is a mode of seduction—one which employs flamboyant mannerisms susceptible of a double interpretation; gestures full of duplicity, with a witty meaning for cognoscenti and another, more impersonal, for outsiders. Equally and by extension, when the word becomes a noun, when a person or a thing is "a camp," duplicity is involved. Behind the "straight" public sense in which something can be taken, one has found a private zany experience of the thing. (110)

This description seems to point toward thinking of camp as a type of performance that perhaps finds its full expression in theater. In its "duplicity," it masquerades important meanings as trivialities (or vice versa). In the post–World War II era, and especially beginning in the 1960s, the theater would become responsive to camp as a way of satirizing American life, but drawing less upon satire's moral force, and more on camp's disreputable, yet comic, reputation for not respecting boundaries.

Who's Afraid of Virginia Woolf? (I am George, I am)

Perhaps the most famous example of camp as theater from this period is Edward Albee's 1962 play, *Who's Afraid of Virginia Woolf?* Albee got his title reportedly from an epithet scrawled on the walls of a Greenwich Village toilet (Sheward 177). The play is about a middle-aged couple, George and Martha, and takes place entirely in their home on a college campus where George is a history professor and Martha is the daughter of the President of the university. A younger couple arrives for nightcaps after a faculty cocktail party, and the four of them drink until dawn, playing various emotional mind games, under the direction of George and Martha. The play has been subject to persistent speculation that the two married couples actually are meant to represent two homosexual couples, and it has also acquired a reputation for its profane (and often bitter) language. The profanity of the dialogue does give the play a punchy, controversial charge. The combination of the cerebral, academic setting with raunchy, outrageous characterizations gives it an unmistakable camp sensibility.

Martha, on whom the play's dynamics operate, best represents this sensibility. Martha is bitter, lecherous, and spoiled, but she is also sharply witty and sensual. Her bitterly raucous marriage to George, in which they both seem to be hopelessly stuck, along with their continual use of bitchy, insulting humor foreshadows *The Boys in the Band*. The character Martha has been described as "really a man in drag" (Harris 96), but instead seems closer to a Tennessee Williams's heroine such as Maggie in *Cat on a Hot Tin Roof*. Martha's fiercely camp persona, along with the tone of the play is set in the opening scene:

> MARTHA: (Looks about the room. Imitates Bette Davis) What a dump. Hey, what's that from? "What a dump!"
> GEORGE: How would I know what . . .
> MARTHA: Aw, come on! What's it from? *You* know . . .
> GEORGE: . . . Martha . . .
> MARTHA: WHAT'S IT FROM, FOR CHRIST'S SAKE?
> GEORGE: (Wearily) What's what from?
> MARTHA: I just told you; I just did it. "What a dump!" Hunh? What that's from?
> GEORGE: I haven't the faintest idea what . . .

MARTHA: Dumbbell! It's from some goddam Bette Davis picture... some goddamn Warner Brothers epic...
GEORGE; *I* can't remember all the pictures that...
MARTHA; Nobody's asking you to remember every single goddamn Warner Brothers epic... just one! One single little epic! Bette Davis gets peritonitis in the end... she's got this big black fright wig she wears all through the picture and she gets peritonitis, and she's married to Joseph Cotten or something... What's the name of the *picture*? I want to know what the name of the *picture* is. She sits down in front of her dressing table... and she's got this peritonitis... and she tries to put her lipstick on, but she can't... and she gets it all over her face... but she decides to go to Chicago anyway, and...
GEORGE: "Chicago"! It's called "Chicago."
MARTHA: Hunh? What... what is?
GEORGE: The picture... it's called "Chicago"...
MARTHA: Good grief! Don't you know anything? "Chicago" was a thirties musical starring little Miss Alice Faye. Don't you know *anything*? (3–5)

This referencing of old movies, the insistence that movie trivia is vitally important information, and the fact that Martha theatrically acts out a gay male icon like Davis are all significant camp markers. As Sontag puts it, camp has a "relish for the exaggeration of sexual characteristics and personality mannerisms. For obvious reasons, the best examples that can be cited are movie stars... The great stylists of temperament and mannerism, like Bette Davis..." (279). Notice, too, Martha's insistence that "I just did it, 'What a dump,'" points to the campy, even drag queen-like device of movie star imitation. Esther Newton notes in *Mother Camp*, that "drag and camp are the most representative and widely used symbols of homosexuality in the English speaking world" (100) and Martha is drawing on both. Albee sets his entire play in motion with this campy gesture—ensuring that this type of mood will be embellished as the play progresses.

It is also the beginning of a game, and it is game playing that dictates the play's form. In the first act, entitled "Fun and Games," George and Martha, as Harold Clurman puts it, engage in a "love-hate dance of death, which they enact in typical American fashion by fun and games swamped in a sauce of strong drink. They bubble and fester with poisonous quips" (482). The atmosphere becomes claustrophobic, and cruelly anarchic, as just about anything gets said, however rude or inappropriate. The various games that George and Martha orchestrate are called

"Humiliate the Host," "Hump the Hostess," and "Get the Guests." Everyone then has an equal chance at humiliation and revelation, until all defenses are unraveled and shells are cast aside. (It's more fun that way, George and Martha seem to suggest.)

Humiliation and Unrequited Love

The echo of Albee's game playing is heard in Crowley's play, in which the game has more obvious effects. The structure of *The Boys in the Band* leads toward a final climax: the playing of "Affairs of the Heart," which has as its central, humiliating premise calling the one person you have ever truly loved. The cruelty and obvious melodrama of the game become manifest in the two most marginal characters of the cast, Bernard and Emory. The game foregrounds how they are not only drawn together in the racial and sexual politics of the play, but also how they are humiliated by more than purely homophobic oppression.

Bernard is coerced into telephoning Peter Dahlbeck, who Emory describes as "the boy in Detroit whose family Bernard's mother has been a laundress for since he was a pickaninny." Bernard explains that he "worked for them too—after school and every summer . . . I think I've loved him all my life. But he never knew I was alive. Besides, he's straight." Bernard reveals that one drunken night they finally had sex in the pool house. Bernard was worried about what straight Peter's reaction would be in the morning, but he pretended that nothing at all had happened. Peter is now married to his third wife, who Bernard knows he has just separated from. When he calls, Peter's mother answers the phone, and Bernard identifies himself as "Bernard—Francine's boy." Emory here corrects him: "Son, not boy." (That Emory would be concerned about Bernard's racial pride seems odd considering his prior remarks.) Bernard continues speaking nervously with Peter's mother and finally hangs up without saying anything revealing, but he is shaken, "Why did I call? Why did I do that?" (77). Bernard will not recover from his phone call for the duration of the play. He is now broken, and no longer participates in any meaningful way with the group.

Michael is disappointed in the outcome of that round and sharply tells Emory to call his great love, Delbert Botts, who Emory "loved since the first day I laid eyes on him when I was in the fifth grade and he was a senior." Delbert eventually becomes a dentist (the others shriek at both his name and his profession) during Emory's senior year in high school. Emory deliberately goes to get his teeth cleaned by him and tells him that he is in charge of decorations for the Prom: "I told him that I was going to burn incense in pots so that white fog would hover the dance floor and it would be like heaven—just like I'd seen it in a Rita Hayworth movie—I can't remember the title." Michael supplies it: "The picture was called *Down to Earth*. Any kid knows that." Delbert doesn't seem impressed by Emory's decorative accomplishments, but Emory is determined to be his friend despite his engagement to a woman, Loraine. Emory calls Delbert to ask if he can see him, and when they meet, Emory reveals his intentions: "I was so nervous this time—my hands were shaking and my voice was unsteady. I couldn't look at him— I just stared straight in space and blurted out why I'd come—I told him . . . I wanted him to be my friend. I said that I never knew anyone who I could talk to and tell everything to and trust. I asked him if he would be my friend." Delbert says yes, and Emory leaves to go buy him a gold lighter with his initials monogrammed on it (81).

Melodramatically, as Emory tells it, he overheard on the night of the Prom, "two girls giggling together. They were standing behind some goddamn corrugated cardboard Greek columns . . . the girl was telling the story . . . her mother had heard it from Loraine's mother. Obviously, Del had told Loraine about the gift. Pretty soon everyone at the dance had heard about it and they were all laughing and making jokes. Everybody knew I had a crush . . . and that I had asked him to be my friend . . . What they didn't know was . . . that I would go on loving him years after they had forgotten my funny secret" (81). It is precisely this type of maudlin speech that critics like Pauline Kael deride:

> The fun of the homosexual vernacular and the interaction of the troupe of actors on-stage helped a little to conceal the play's mechanics, in which each reveals 'the truth' about himself . . . but Friedkin, by limiting the number of actors in the frame to those directly involved in the dialogue and by the insistence of his close-ups, forces our attention to the pity-of-it-all. When the camera slowly moves in for the emotional kill as Emory/Emily talks about how the kids at school made fun of him, one's thoughts drift back to "East Lynne" and other works of cool sophistication. (173–174)

Interestingly, Harold also remarks on the sentimentality of Emory's story: "Well, I for one need an insulin injection." Within the drama itself, there is a recognition that certain expressions of emotion are not even appropriate to camp, and that they don't have enough irony or emotional distance to sustain comic interest. Kael's reference to a crudely melodramatic British serial is especially cutting, since she finds even *that* more palatable than Emory's story. But how should Emory have told his story? He has the most developed camp sensibility of the bunch and this may preclude him from having any feelings at all that are not mediated by camp. His own investment in camp has not allowed him any degree of seriousness, now at his own expense. As we shall see, this is an example of too quickly foreclosing the parameters of camp.

Bernard begs Emory not to call, not to humiliate himself, and when Emory claims that he has nothing to lose, Bernard replies, "Your dignity. That's what you've got to lose." This leads to the most interesting and confusing exchange in the entire play:

> MICHAEL: Well, that's a knee-slapper! I love your telling him about dignity when you allow him to degrade you constantly by Uncle Tom-ing you to death.
> BERNARD: He can do it, Michael. I can do it. But you can't do it.
> MICHAEL: Isn't that discrimination?
> BERNARD: I don't like it from him and I don't like it from me—but I do it to myself and I let him do it. I let him do it because it's the only thing, to him, makes him my equal. We both got the short end of the stick—but I got a hell of a lot more than he did and he knows it. So, I let him Uncle Tom me just so he can tell himself he's not a complete loser.
> MICHAEL: How very considerate.
> BERNARD: It's his defense. You have your defense, Michael. But it's indescribable. (85)

Bernard and Emory's humiliation in this game is contrasted with Hank and Larry, who in a pique of sentimentality call each other to express their love. Hank and Larry, despite issues of jealousy, are held up as the paragon of stability, enforced by their "straight-acting" appearances. But Emory also reaches a climax of reconciliation with Bernard, where he seems to realize the offensiveness of his racial insults. That this moment—however dramatically manipulated—is allowed to happen at all is testament not necessarily to the anti-racist potential of the play, but instead to the very recognition that some things can be unacceptable or harmful in the "grammar of camp."

This is a hopeful sign in the play, however unimposing it seems, but it is interesting that this type of reconciliation is seemingly not possible within the context of camp. It is only by dis-inhabiting campiness that this important, serious moment can occur. Emory is only able to achieve understanding and compassion by somehow being not so "Emory" anymore. Bernard is able to reveal himself and explain his relationship with Emory, only in a context of complete pity and self-loathing. In the midst of this scene, Michael is still participating in racist camping and so remains oblivious to, and apart from, the transcendence that the mechanics of the play value.

However, the sentimentality of this moment is perhaps not so clearly delineated from camp. In Albee's play, Martha and George, after many hours of tortuous, painful (and often humorous) games, look out the window at the dawn, and seem to realize—broken and defeated—that they have only each other. Their murderous and insanely staged fights leave them spent and exhausted (as is the audience). But then when George asks, "Who's Afraid of Virginia Woolf?" Martha answers with the last words of the play, "I am, George, I am." Albee undercuts the emotional devastation of his play with a literary allusion and seems to escape the maudlin in a deliberate, yet elliptical way, while Crowley bluntly, does not. But if Albee's play is clearly the more artful, and more aesthetically and historically significant than Crowley's, it is less attentive to the messiness and emotional entanglements of history. Crowley's clumsy dramaturgy and obvious melodramatic effects in a sense "act out" an important aspect of camp's function: a valuing of the intense emotions that living on the margins can produce.

Bernard and Emory's experiences represent two models of unrequited love. Bernard loves Peter, who because of class, caste, and sexual orientation cannot reciprocate Bernard's love. Peter will remain Bernard's great love—which may in some way be predicated on these very exclusions. Emory's love is also separated from him by external circumstances: Delbert is aggressively heterosexual, having married several times and practices a most "un-Emory" profession, dentistry. Do Bernard and Emory practice a form of masochism in their investments in true love? Do they prize only what is unattainable to them? I'd like to think of a way through these questions that does not rely on moralistic value judgments, or on disempowering two already marginal figures. Therefore, I'd like to consider carefully the relationship between camp and sentimentality.

Camp and Sentimentality

In the play, Emory embodies camp and its functions and is punished within the text as such. Bernard is often the target of camp, but he also represents a marginality within another marginality. This links him to Emory conclusively within the dynamics of the play. Emory is marginal because of his effeminacy, Bernard because of his race. The fact that their quests for love are failures—failures they cannot seem to forget—is linked to their respective marginalization.

In a social context in which "love" is made manifest by reciprocal institutional commitments, such as marriage, along with the prohibitions of class, race, and sexuality, Bernard and Emory lose on all counts. They, however, seem to believe most fervently in the ideal of a "true love," even while characters such as straight-acting Larry disparage such bourgeois fantasies. (Larry can afford to.) Their ability—however damaging to their psyches—to construct scenarios of beauty and love in such dire emotional circumstances, is a tribute to their abilities to fashion and refashion their emotional investments. I don't think, then, that their campiness is all that is extended in this final scene. Camp allows them not to accept the "reality" of their love and gives them the space to exaggerate—to dramatically stage—what really are scenes of maudlin self-pity and failed love.

But why is this significant? That love fails, that love operates unfairly and unevenly is a fairly pedestrian observation. It is not the "facts" of love that matter in this case, what matters is the decorative embroidery that Bernard and Emory craft around what seem to be trivial experiences. It is their ability to value what should probably be thrown away as valueless that makes them expert practitioners of camp. They insist on the seriousness of their impossible investments, are seemingly oblivious to irony (reality made humorous), and are willing to be reckless and miserable for what they see as love. They are also refusing to incorporate the limitations imposed upon them by historical circumstances. They are not unaware of history, of caste, of class, but they operate their emotional lives despite these immutable oppressions. Crowley allows these characters to inhabit their loss, and this makes the play camp, but in a much less obvious way.

This may be hard to reconcile with the most widely circulated definitions of camp which characterize a camp attitude as consisting of a detached irony toward its object of consideration. A camp attitude in this sense refuses to take anything too seriously. But as Sontag explains, camp is not about feeling superior to a representation:

> Camp taste, is, above all, a mode of enjoyment, of appreciation—not judgment . . . it doesn't sneer at someone who succeeds in being seriously dramatic. What it does is to find the success in certain passionate failures. Camp taste is a kind of love, love for human nature. It relishes rather than judges, the little triumphs and awkward intensities of "character" . . . Camp taste identifies with what it is enjoying. People who share this sensibility are not laughing at the thing they label as "a camp," they are enjoying it. Camp is a tender feeling. (292)

I argue it is the very pathos of emotional loss and even devastation that not only contains important components of camp, but also important "political" considerations. By this I mean that the definition of "political" should include discussions of emotional investments—since these investments always take place in a context of historical forces. If camp reminds us to value the trivial, to look again at the waste of consumerism, to take images in bad Hollywood movies seriously, it can also teach us to take the world of melodrama as containing kernels of historical truth and the historical effects of oppression. In this sense, Crowley's play is important to queer culture and the culture of feeling, as it runs through the effects of loss, bitterness, and heartbreak, in a specific historical formation.

The Boys in the Band was staged in what was almost the night before Stonewall. That Stonewall would raise questions of sexuality and equal rights did not mean that it would resolve them, or even that it had invented these questions. Richard Dyer describes the "camp sensibility" as being "very much a product of our oppression. And inevitably, it is scarred by that oppression" (144–145). But scars and all, camp offers a way of reexamining questions of race and culture, not to mention sentimentality and loss. In the next section, I discuss these concerns further, but for now, it is important to see *The Boys in the Band* as an attempt at dramatizing the power and contradictions of camp. That it may not have been entirely successful or artful does not detract from its importance historically for gay male culture, especially as it opened up questions of identity and emotional loss.

Chapter 2
"Letting Go of What You Love": Literature, Popular Culture, and Chicano Heartache

Drawing on the previous discussion of camp and its connection to both the comic and the sentimental, I would like to move the discussion to texts that deal more specifically with the borderlands of race and sexuality. Beginning with a short story, "Bien Pretty," from Sandra Cisneros' collection, *Woman Hollering Creek and Other Stories*, I set the groundwork for a discussion on the everyday uses of popular culture and sentimentality and their relationship to a racialized Chicana/o sexuality. From this, the focus of the chapter moves to Arturo Islas' novel *Migrant Souls*, which plays with the sentimental and the historical while coding the homosexuality present throughout the text. The goal of this chapter is to foreground the relationship between what Eve Kosofsky Sedgwick in *The Epistemology of the Closet* describes as the "spectacle of the closet" and questions of race and culture.

Chicano Identity

Literary critic, Ramon Saldívar, in *Chicano Narrative: The Dialectics of Difference* describes identity in Chicano narrative as not "unified and linear," but instead "complexly dialectical, without coalescence or synthesis. It establishes itself continuously on the unstable borderline of difference between Mexican and American social ideologies and expresses itself as the historical working out of the contradictions implicit in both the Mexican and American ethical, cultural, and political economies . . . [it] is both Mexican and American and also neither one nor the other, completely. It remains on the precarious utopian margin between the two, perhaps as the very sign of marginality institutionalized in geopolitical terms by the border between the sovereign states of Mexico and the United States" (174–175). The "utopian margin" Saldívar cites is precisely the topography this book inhabits. Importantly, Saldívar introduces a discussion on texts by Chicana writers by describing these women writers as not only challenging the "resistance to dominant ideologies initiated by male authors" but also "adding both male/female and hetero-/homosexual binarisms to the discussion of the social construction of a Chicano identity" (175).

This space opened by the challenges of Chicana feminism's social, sexual, and creative productions, is the setting in which I want to discuss "Bien Pretty" and *Migrant Souls*. These two texts' relationship to autobiography (or semi-autobiography) is mediated by their relationship to culture and specific cultural artifacts, along with their respective sexualities. In these works, binaries such as public/private, authentic/artificial, and past/present are imaginatively challenged and even the terms are transformed. The characters suffer in love in deeply transforming ways and are impacted by history in the most private regions of their hearts.

"Bien Pretty"

Sandra Cisneros' short story, "Bien Pretty" was published in 1991 in her collection *Woman Hollering Creek and Other Stories*. It is a different kind of love story. In it, Lupe Arrendondo has moved from San Francisco to San Antonio to house sit for her friend, Irasema Izaura Coronado, a "famous Texas poet who carries herself as if she is directly descended from Ixtaccihuatl." Lupe house-sits along with (I quote only a portion of the complete list):

> (8) Oaxacan black pottery pieces
> signed Diego Rivera monotype
> Star-shaped piñata
> (5) strings of red chile lights
> antique Spanish shawl
> cappuccino maker
> replica of the goddess Catlicue
> life-size papier mache skeleton signed by the Linares family
> Frida Kahlo altar
> Punched tin Virgen de Guadalupe chandelier
> bent-twig couch with Mexican serape
> eye-of-God crucifix
> knotty pine armoire
> death mask of Pancho Villa with mouth slightly open . . . (139–140)

The story is populated with such lists; they operate in Fredric Jameson's terms as "pastiche" and as a device of postmodernism, with its endless list of objects and references to various historical and cultural moments. Each of the lists in the story operates as a signifier; from this list we are to gather that the house owners are educated enough to know both the necessities of Latino cultural authenticity (Frida Kahlo altar) and the necessities of bourgeois comfort (cappuccino maker). Cisneros uses these lists in a deftly satirical manner, drawing comedy from the odd juxtapositions, but as we shall see, the joke is eventually on the wry protagonist.

Lupe brings with her from Northern California: "A futon. A stainless steel wok. My grandmother's molcajete. A pair of flamenco shoes ... Eleven huipiles ... My Tae Kwon Do uniform. My crystals and copal ..." (141). This is a truly postmodern group of signifiers that could perhaps only have come from the Bay Area, with its celebrated fusion of cultures from around the globe. There is a combination of different cultural practices that describes someone who can move easily from one cultural value to another as the purpose suits her. It also points toward a "New Age" identity, combining indigenous fetishization with cultural privilege. The comic juxtapositions suggest also Sontag's (and others) list of camp objects and this "campiness" in assembling markers of cultural authenticity is present throughout the story.

The story is sent into motion when under "this veneer of Southwest funk, of lace and silk, and porcelain, beyond the embroidered pillows that said DUERME, MI AMOR, the Egyptian cotton sheets and eyelet bedspread ... the gilt edged tea set, the abalone-handled silver, the obsidian hair combs, the sticky, cough-medicine-and-powdered sugar," Lupe finds a number of unglamorous, Texas-sized cockroaches (140). She goes into some detail describing the insects, concentrating especially on the sounds they make during the night. Lupe's roach problem will not sound unfamiliar to anyone who has spent any amount of time in Texas, but it represents something more. There are two symbols at work here—cockroaches and Texas.

Cockroaches have played an important role in the popular imaginary of Chicano culture for ages. From the stereotypical musical strains of "La Cucaracha" in 1930s Hollywood movies such as *Viva Villa!* (1934) when a Latino character appears to Acosta's *Revolt of the Cockroach People*, this brown, persistently hardy creature has haunted representations of Chicanos and Latinos. As for Texas, it operates in the story as a symbol of excess since everything exists there in gargantuan proportions, whether it be cockroaches or racism. Lupe's friend warns her before her move from sophisticated San Francisco: "Lupe, are you crazy? They still lynch Meskins down there. Everybody's got chain saws and gun racks and pickups and Confederate flags. Aren't you scared?" If California represents a measure of racial tolerance, Texas represents the exact opposite. In this sense, what happens to Lupe while she is in Texas is constituted as more "real world" than her experiences in the West; furthermore, unlike in California, while she is in Texas, she is confronted by contradictions about her identity and "authenticity." What pushes her to take residence in San Antonio is a bad breakup with her boyfriend, Eddie, who she says left her for a "blonde . . . He didn't even have the decency to pick a woman of color" (142). Lupe finds herself in a different type of sexual and racial complication in Texas which all begins because of a roach infestation.

Prince Popo in Texas

Having had enough of flying roaches, she calls an exterminator, "La Cucaracha Apachurrada Pest Control" to take care of her problem. As she checks out the exterminator, Flavio Manguia, she decides that he would make a "perfect Prince Popo for a painting" she had been thinking about. Lupe explains: "I'd always wanted to do an updated version of the Prince Popocatepetl/Princess Ixtaccihuatl volcano myth, that tragic love story metamorphosized from classic to kitsch calendar art, like the ones you get at Carniceria Ximenez or Tortilleria la Guadalupanita. Prince Popo, half-naked Indian warrior built like Johnny Weismuller, crouched in grief beside his sleeping princess Ixtaccihuatl, buxom as an Indian Jayne Mansfield. And behind them, echoing their silhouettes, their namesake volcanoes" (144). Lupe's idea for an artpiece is based on wanting to "metamorphosize" what has become a cliché into art. Her being sexually drawn to Flavio as her model provides the impetus for this metamorphosis. However, in a constant thematic throughout the story, Lupe seems to sense that she inhabits a cultural space of self-conscious cultural appropriation. In her incessant list making and descriptions of cultural artifacts, the text foregrounds the construction of Lupe's identity. In the story, however, the banality of an "identity" being "constructed" is offset by the role of love and sexual passion in the text.

On Lupe's first date with Flavio she made a "wonderful paella with brown rice and tofu and a pitcher of fresh sangria. Gipsy Kings were on the tape recorder. [She] wore her Lycra mini, a pair of silver cowboy boots, and a fringed shawl across my Danskin like Carmen in that film by Carlos Saura." Every cliché of Spanish/Latino life is realized in Lupe's careful preparations. But it is at dinner that Lupe outdoes herself with overly-educated, multicultural prattle: "I talked about how I once had my aura massaged by an Oakland curandera, Afro-Brazilian dance as a means of spiritual healing, where I might find good dim sum in San Antonio, and whether a white woman has the right to claim to be an Indian shamaness" (150). Flavio, in turn, responds in authentic, working-class Chicano/Mexicano chatter:

> Flavio talked about how Alex El Guero from work had won a Sony boom box that morning just by being the ninth caller on 107 FM K-Suave, how his Tia Tencha makes the best tripe soup ever no lie, how before leaving Corpus he and Johnny Canales from El Show de Johnny Canales had been like this until a bet over Los Bukis left them not speaking to each other, how every Thursday night he works out at a gym on Calaveras with aims to build himself a body better than Mil Mascara's, and is there an English equivalent for the term "la fulana"? (150)

Class and race inflect each of the referents Lupe and Flavio use; each is speaking "truthfully" from his/her own experiences and concerns. But Lupe's talk sounds positively comic next to Flavio's chatter, which is comic in a different way. While he seems to be speaking unpretentiously, therefore giving an amusing tenderness to his aspirations, Lupe sounds silly and pretentious, trying to make pithy observations about literally a world of topics. She is overreaching to be something she is not, so she sounds hollow and flat. Flavio's speech, especially when read aloud, has wonderful rhythms, and seems endearing and "real." In this, Flavio is contrasted with Lupe's bourgeois multiculturalism.

Sexual Authenticity

The most illuminating scene in the story takes place after dinner when Lupe asks Flavio, "Who dresses you?" Flavio replies that his cousin Silver does, and Lupe states with all her cultural and political authority, "What you are, sweetheart, is a product of American imperialism." She then reaches over to "pluck at the alligator on his shirt." Flavio replies, "I don't have to dress in a serape and sombrero to be Mexican . . . I know who I am." Lupe's reaction is decidedly mixed: "I wanted to leap across the table, throw the Oaxacan black pottery pieces across the room, swing from the punched tin chandelier, fire a pistol at his Reeboks and force him to dance. I wanted to be Mexican at that moment but it was true. I was not Mexican" (151–152). If Lupe is not Mexican, what is she? Her realization that her identity is not what she desperately wants it to be, that she is not "authentically" Mexican, results in her becoming sexually attracted to what she sees Flavio as embodying. Lupe's upbringing and education have caused her to lose something. Lupe seeks to heal this loss through Flavio. He is not a Gypsy Kings tape, he is the real thing. Her sexual desire for him is mainly constructed on his perceived cultural authenticity:

> I'd never made love in Spanish before. I mean not with anyone whose first language was Spanish. There was crazy Graham . . . but he was Welsh . . . and Eddie, sure. But Eddie and I were products of our American education. Anything tender always came off sounding like the subtitles to a Buñuel film. But Flavio . . . To make love in Spanish, in a manner as intricate and devout as la Alhambra. To have a lover sigh *mi vida, mi preciosa, mi chiquitita*, and whisper things in that language crooned to babies, that language murmured by grandmothers, those words that smelled like your house, like flour tortillas, and the inside of your daddy's hat, like everyone talking in the kitchen at the same time . . . That language. That sweep of palm leaves and fringed shawls. That startled fluttering, like the heart of a goldfinch or fan . . . How could I think of making love in English again? (153)

Here, language with its particular associations is directly linked to desire. Lupe re-associates images from the past, from her childhood, with her sexual pleasure. Sexual desire is linked to memory, to recognition of a lost cultural past. The memory that is evoked for her consists of fairly conventional images that acquire a more profound meaning for their having to be retrieved. Her language, her Spanish, her infancy, her grandmother, her father, her home, all of these images come flooding back like a sexual and verbal "madeline." (Proust will reappear later in Islas' novels, with their blending of autobiography, fiction, and history.) That her "culture" and her past can be retrieved by an insect exterminator adds to the pathos, to the mundanity of her situation. What is important here is that Cisneros is describing a recuperation of a past and an identity through sexual pleasure.

That a privileged, educated woman of color is sexually objectifying Flavio is a fairly obvious point. What is notable here is the curious circulation of gender and racial politics. If Cisneros is slyly satirizing a particular historical moment in Chicano history—a moment in which assimilation, politicization, and authenticity are not clearly delineated taxonomies—she is also describing a moment in which feminism has made particular articulations of desire allowable. Lupe is "in charge" of her narrative, and she sets out in the story to acquire her desires, on her own terms, but somehow they always escape her grasp.

It is interesting, too, that the middle-class "inauthentic" figure in the story is a woman, and that the "real" figure is a man. Feminists of color have noted the fact that U.S. cultural nationalisms from the 1960s, black and Chicano especially, relied heavily on masculinist representations. As Cherrie Moraga argues, "What was right about Chicano Nationalism was its commitment to preserving the integrity of the Chicano people ... What was wrong about Chicano nationalism was its institutionalized heterosexism, its inbred machismo..." (148–149). But what Cisneros is complicating is a particular articulation of desire on the part of a heterosexual woman for a particular articulation of masculinist nationalism. This seems to formulate desire as consisting of what is lacking in oneself, and in a heterosexist, masculinist culture, this will, obviously, tend to be heterosexual desire. Or it could point to the continual frustration of such a desire. In other words, one can never *be* what one desires, but it's this failed aspiration which fuels the sexual connection in the story. Lupe desires Flavio even more for what he is, what he embodies, and what she feels she has lost.

Lupe's affair with Flavio is inevitably doomed; he has to leave to care for his two wives and children from other assorted women. Lupe is crushed. She tries an elaborate series of magical and herbal spells, which she buys from "Casa Preciado Religious Articles, the Mexican voodoo shop on South Laredo." At the store she sees: "Magic oils, magic perfume and soaps, votive candles, milagritos, holy cards, magnet car-statuettes, plaster saints with eyelashes made from human hair, San Martin Caballero good-luck horseshoes, incense and copal, aloe vera bunched, blessed, bound with red string ... Herbs stocked from floor to ceiling in labeled drawers: AGUACATE, ALBAHACA, ALTAMISA, ANACAHUITE, BARBAS DE ELOTE, CEDRON DE CASTILLO, COYOTE, CHARRASQUILLA..." (159). These various objects contain the historical encounters between indigenous and Catholic belief systems; they also represent the encounter between religious faith and superstitious consumerism. Lupe describes choosing a candle from the "pagan side" as well as a "Virgen de Guadalupe from the Christian." Seen one way, this could represent the kitsch aspect of religious paraphernalia, of which Catholicism abounds. But this combination of pagan and Christian is one that Lupe knows, historically, she must participate in; the fairly obvious "silliness" behind thinking these candles can work is undercut by the historical necessity of having to identify a "pagan" and a "Christian."

Lupe wonders, "These candles and yerbas and stuff, do they really work?" Whether or not they work, Lupe seems right in pursuing a solution for her romantic predicament from the Mexican voodoo shop, if what she finds there is viewed as an aspect of popular culture. In this sense I mean to define popular culture as what is most available and what is created and consumed out of a historical and material reality. It also means a relief from the solemnity and gravity of not only high culture, but in this instance, from religious institutions. Most importantly, perhaps, popular culture is a release from societal expectations of discipline and emotional rationality. Lupe doubts whether burning a powder, "Regrase a mi" ("Come back to me"), will in fact bring Flavio back, but she participates in the ritual anyway. The suspension of disbelief performed in this magical/religious ritual is not unlike that performed by a cultural critic's faith in the potency of popular culture to effect social transformation.

Amar es Vivir

Lupe's revelation and salvation do not, however, come through these magic items, but come instead via the most sturdy of Chicano/Latino institutions—the *telenovela*, or soap opera. She plans her days around these programs: "Avoiding board meetings, rushing home from work . . . Just so I could be seated in front of the screen in time to catch *Rosa Salvaje* with Veronica Castro . . . Or Daniela Romo in *Balada por un Amor*. Or Adela Noriega in *Dulce Desafio*. I watched them all. In the name of research." But her research leaves her unhappy with the women she sees on the *telenovelas*. She starts to have dreams "of these Rosas and Briandas and Luceros. And in my dreams I'm slapping the heroine to her senses, because I want them to be women who make things happen, not women who things happen to . . . Real women. The ones I've loved all my life . . . The ones I've known everywhere except on TV, in books and magazines. *Las girlfriends. Las comadres.* Our *mamas* and *tias*. Passionate *and* powerful, tender and volatile, brave. And, above all, fierce" (161). The solace she finds in the melodramatic entanglements of the soap operas is compromised by what she knows are one-dimensional representations of women. Then why is she irresistibly drawn to these representations nonetheless? Like most emotional investments that Lupe makes, this one is also steeped in passionate ambivalence.

In the next scene, a cashier at the grocery store is ringing her up, and notices that Lupe is buying *Vanidades*, a popular magazine detailing the exploits of all the hottest *telenovela* stars. The cashier and she exchange pop culture pleasantries, the cashier notices the star on the cover of the magazine, Libertad Palomares. This causes Lupe to muse: "Libertad

Palomares. A big Venezuelan *telenovela* star. Big on crying. Every episode she weeps like a Magdalene. Not me. I couldn't cry if my life depended on it" (162). They both discuss how they never miss an episode, and the cashier, who is described as looking "old. Tired. Never mind the red lips, the eye makeup that just makes her look sad. Those creases from the corner of the lip to the wing of the nostril from holding in anger, or tears. Or both," tells her she hopes she gets home from work in time to watch it.

It is through this exchange at the end of the story, in which Lupe recognizes both the cashier's economic limitations and her own emotional despair, that she finds the key:

> *Amar es Vivir.* [To love is to live.] What it comes down to for that woman at Centano's and for me. It was enough to keep us tuning in every day at six-thirty, another episode, another thrill. To relive that living when the universe ran through the blood like river water. Alive. Not the weeks spent writing grant proposals, not the forty hours standing behind a cash register shoving cans of refried beans into plastic sacks. Hell, no. This wasn't what we were put on the planet for. Not ever. (163)

The material realities of grant proposals and sacking groceries cannot compete with the vision that Lupe conjures up. The state of "living" is highlighted as existing apart from what constitutes everyday reality. In this sense, the soap opera contains the vital ingredients of life. In this context, it is laboring in empty enterprises that starves the soul and is false and inhuman.

If Lupe has wanted her *telenovela* heroines to be more explicitly assertive, she has also come to see the power in popular culture. Her stirring revelation, in fact, is written at the fevered pitch in which an actress delivers her final salvo before the curtain closes: "One way or another. Even if it's only the lyrics to a stupid pop hit. We're going to right the world and live. I mean live our lives the way lives were meant to be lived. With the throat and wrists. With rage and desire, and joy and grief, and love til it hurts, maybe. But goddamn, girl. Live" (163). It is as if Lupe has realized that however degrading daily work can be, however much expectations of love may be unmet in a world dominated by oppressive forms of repression (racism, capitalism, sexism), that to be fully "alive," one needs to engage in human contact, in love and desire, however sorrowful the outcome.

It is my contention that those with the least power at their disposal often make "love" and suffering into practically a sacrament. But it is also my contention that this is not solely a matter of recompense. The lyrics to the stupid pop hit do contain a power that Lupe finally recognizes. The empowerment that Lupe experiences at the end of the story is also a realization of her connection to her culture and to her past. Her unrequited love for Flavio, was based on what she saw as her own unrequited relationship to feeling "Mexican." This suddenly seems less important upon her recognition that she is most fully alive through a thoroughly "Mexican" characteristic—however stereotypically drawn— "suffering through love."

Where Migrant Souls Go

I discuss the Cisneros story in order to introduce a novel that was published in 1990, *Migrant Souls* by Arturo Islas. The novel can be described as a comedy about suffering: a comedy because the characters cling to suffering as a religion, as an art form, as a way of life. It takes place in El Paso, flashing through time from the 1950s onward. In the novel, history and the past become an overpowering force that various characters valiantly, yet helplessly, struggle against. *Migrant Souls* is at once an autobiography and a fiction, caught somewhere in-between the two, a familiar space in Islas' writings, and an echo of Proust. His writings mix chronology and memory, piecing together the story of the Angel family as it would be remembered, as it would be lived, and not as it may have "really" happened.

The novel is a sequel to (and a rewriting of) his previous book, *The Rain God*, published in 1984. While these two books are different in scope and reach, they both feature the same main character, Miguel Chico, and share an oblique relationship to homosexuality. As we shall see, homosexuality is present throughout the novel, yet it is hardly mentioned or named as such. In particular ways, Catholicism becomes the guiding force, and its seeming incompatibility with homosexuality adds to the melancholic and incomplete tone of the story. It is because of Catholicism that the Chicano protagonist cannot visibly "come out." But it is also because of Catholicism that he ably inhabits a space of self-suffering and is capable of grandiloquent, melodramatic gestures. These gestures are beautifully campy and "gay," yet they owe their existence to the prohibition on gayness. That out of this mountainous Catholic repression, Islas is able to craft a lushly historical Chicano gay narrative is just one of the major maneuvers the book makes toward imaginative irreconciliation.

The Chicano Closet and Islas' Sexuality

In the heading under "Latino Literature" in the encyclopedic *Gay and Lesbian Heritage: A Reader's Companion*, a question is raised: "Why are there so few published works by Latino gay men?" The article poses the question considering the "proliferation of a Chicano literary renaissance in the wake of the Chicano movement of the 1960s," and the appearance of texts, "both fictional and theoretical by Chicana and Latina lesbian writers of the 1980s."

Four reasons are offered to explain the paucity of gay Latino texts: machismo, Catholicism, racism, and AIDS. Machismo is described as "omnipresent" in the culture with Latinos having a "hyperinvestment" in perpetuating traditional gender roles. Catholicism is seen as having a "monumental" influence, increasing the difficulty of shaping a gay identity. Racism makes it difficult for Latino writers to get published because their work is either too ethnic, or not ethnic enough. AIDS is melodramatically described as having "decimated the Latino gay male population in the United States." The hyperbolic sentiment of some of these statements aside, the factors listed have indeed accounted for the dearth of texts available about the Chicano/Latino gay experience (436).

What these four factors create, in a sense, is the "Chicano closet," a space generated because of various historical conditions, which include those listed above, along with political disenfranchisement. Indeed, each of these have impacted gay Chicanos in specific ways, and it seems inevitable that a particular kind of closet would be generated that would contain its own characteristics. I admit I was surprised to see Arturo Islas listed in the *Companion*. His homosexuality still seems to be more a matter of speculation than of "fact." (Which, of course, may be expected and inherent in a homophobic society.) In a piece entitled, "Queer Aztlan," Cherrie Moraga writes about the possibility of creating "queerness" in a Chicano identity. Moraga discusses the impact of AIDS on gay Chicanos and writes,

> Unlike the queens who have always been open about their sexuality, "passing" gay men have learned in a visceral way that being in "the closet" and preserving their "manly" image will not protect them, it will only make their dying more secret. I remember my friend Arturo Islas, the novelist. I think of how his writing begged to boldly announce his gayness. Instead, we learned it through vague references about "sinners" and tortured alcoholic characters who wanted nothing more than to "die dancing" beneath a lightning charged sky just before a thunderstorm. Islas died of AIDS-related illness in 1990, having barely begun to examine the complexity of Chicano sexuality in his writing. (1993: 63)

This is a powerful indictment, Moraga's friendship with Islas notwithstanding. Moraga seems to hold Islas' closetedness responsible not only for his "vague" writing, filled with self-loathing, self-destructive characters, but seemingly also for his own death. For any writer the matter of form reflects upon their thematic and stylistic concerns. For Islas, his novelistic form becomes implicated in his inability to "speak" his personal truths. The novel's artful opacity for Moraga instead becomes a political indictment against Islas. This, though, obscures too much of the productive ambivalence of Islas' work, which redevelops narrative in competing realities.

In Islas, the closet is in fact often wrapped up in a version of a redemptive narrative. The coming out process promises a salvation of identity, in which mysteries are explained and neuroses is evaporated. Representatively, Michelangelo Signorile's *Queer in America: Sex, the Media and the Closets of Power* contains narrative after narrative of the lost soul who finally emerges from the destructive closet and is accountable to his life and the gay community. One story will stand in for many others in his book: Jacques Rosan is introduced as a gay man presently in his thirties who lives in Los Angeles. About ten years previously, however, he had been trying to get work as an actor and a model, eventually becoming an agent where he found himself lying about himself in closeted Hollywood. He hated what he was doing, since he had been out for several years previously, but he felt he had no other options. He began drinking heavily and using cocaine. Then he realized he was "destroying himself. He insists it 'was all because of the closet.' He left the business, sought counseling, and took a job at Greenpeace, where he is open about his homosexuality. Almost immediately, he says, he was able to stop his self-destructive habits" (271–272). This link between self-destruction, a tortured gay identity, and Hollywood was present in the discussion of *The Boys in the Band* and in Moraga's story about Islas, since after Stonewall, the affirmation, "Gay is Good," supposedly alleviated the stigmatizing effect. This idea that emerging out of the closet will, in a sense, clear up the skin, is omnipresent in gay political contemporary culture, and perhaps for good reason. It is in the self-identifying, and in the identifying with a larger community, that often some peace, solace, and even politics can be achieved. But is it enough?

That coming out of the closet will make certain questions about one's identity less opaque is unquestionable. That it will somehow make all questions and self-doubt disappear is absurd. Closets are varied, multiple, and capable of regeneration. Various forces of history and race mediated Islas' particular closet, which lend his writings a unique poignancy. His own writings and teachings reflect a deep commitment to understanding historical formations. But what else is at stake is his identity as a writer of fiction. In this, his closetedness about his gay identity begins to parallel the closetedness in his novels. Islas' writing is filled with vague references to himself, his life, his background, along with his sexuality. At times, it seems a type of textual coyness, a withholding of the obvious, with a teasing amount of information, just enough to be clear as to what is being described while retaining enough textual mystification to make it "fictional." Miguel Chico ends up moving from Del Sapo ("El Paso") to Northern California, becoming an English professor at a prestigious university (unnamed, but clearly Stanford), and writing a novel populated by a family closely resembling his own, narrated by a closeted gay man, who is an English professor at a prestigious university, who closely resembles Islas.

The protagonist's resemblance to Islas himself is as astute an observation as suspecting that Proust's narrator resembles Proust. This open secret of textuality and sexuality is observed quite openly: "Miguel Chico's novel had been written during a sabbatical leave when he decided to make fiction instead of criticize it. A modest, semi-autobiographical work, it was published by a small California press that quickly went out of business. *Tlaloc* was an academic, if not commercial success and its author became known as the ethnic writer. After seeing what the world did to books, he returned humbly to the classroom and to criticism" (210). Islas, in fact, attended Stanford University both as an undergraduate and graduate student, and eventually taught literature and creative writing there until his death. That we "know" the university is Stanford in the novel is part of the game, but importantly, it never figures in the text except as a place where Miguel Chico goes and stays. "Stanford" envelops him as surely as his family and home do, becoming another part of the closet.

Published Islas

Critic Jose David Saldívar, describes Islas' struggle to get his first novel, *The Rain God (Tlaloc)* published: "But after eight years of struggle with unresponsive New York publishing houses (he submitted his novel to more than twenty) he gave up trying to convince them that his story about the Angel family would have 'universal appeal.'" Islas is quoted as saying, "I finally decided to stop banging my head against the wall." Frances McCullough, senior editor at Harper and Row, in a letter to Islas' agent about *The Rain God*, is quoted as writing, "I think what's wrong with the characters is that they are so busy conveying a cultural message that they have no time to be real people. This is true also of the plot; whatever happens has a heavy cultural message but you don't feel its weight in terms of the people's lives." A small Palo Alto publisher, Alexandrian Press, finally published the novel in 1984, but the press eventually shut down (108).

Islas' problems in getting his work published have a familiar poignancy. The difficulty of any writer is to find a responsive and sympathetic publisher (not to mention readers), and for a writer of color the difficulty is manifold. Islas must have felt doubly rejected since the story being turned down as unpublishable was so markedly his own. But what else is telling about the senior editor's callous remarks, is her contention that the characters in Islas' novel are "so busy conveying a cultural message that they have no time to be real people." From a different, unintended perspective, this is precisely what the characters in Islas are suffering from: the heavy burdens of history and "culture" that have prevented them from being, what would be McCullough's eyes, "real people." Islas, in his professional and creative life may have been too astute to believe that history (or the closet) was something that could be emerged from completely.

Parallels

Islas' two novels are described in the *Companion* as focusing on the "life and times of Miguel Chico, a closeted Chicano gay man . . . the novels focus on Chico's struggles to form an identity that will resolve the tensions of his conservative Southwest Latino heritage and his new life in the gay urban culture of San Francisco" (436). But neither of Islas' novels really focuses on Miguel Chico's struggle to form any type of definite identity. As far as the "gay urban culture of San Francisco," Chico never mentions or goes anywhere near a gay neighborhood or has any connection at all with a gay community. But then, he does have two personally crucial gay connections: his married uncle Felix who is brutally murdered by a young soldier he tries to seduce, and a business student Miguel Chico falls in love and lives with in San Francisco, until he is left by his lover's ambitions on the East Coast. *Migrant Souls* is infused with mourning for this love affair which causes him a great deal of emotional and even physical pain. The novel is an attempt to understand the meaning behind emotional, personal suffering over love, and an exploration of unrequited love, as both beautiful and terrible. The novel places this suffering in a historical and a cultural context, where it makes more, or a different kind of "sense." Disappointment in love functions in the novel as a cultural formation from which characters are unable, or even unwilling, to remove themselves. What adds to the melancholy is, of course, the closet, the Chicano closet, where suffering must be done in silence, where men cannot weep over other men, but at the same time where emotions are valued as profoundly life altering. Yet, out of this, like Lupe in Cisneros' story, the characters creatively transform the popular culture around them, turning the movies and even the Catholic Church into tools of survival.

Both *The Rain God* and *Migrant Souls* take as their broad subject the Angel family, led by Mama Chona, who never lets her children and grandchildren forget the story of their family's escape from the Mexican Revolution to El Paso: "The Rio Grande . . . was a constant disappointment and hardly a symbol of the promised land to families like Mama Chona's. They had not sailed across an ocean or ridden wagons and trains across half a continent in search of a new life. They were migrant, not immigrant souls. They simply and naturally went from one bloody side of the river to the other and into a land that just a few decades earlier had been Mexico. They became border Mexicans with American citizenship." Mama Chona is described as feeling the "force of these historical conditions," and is determined that the family, now settled in the United States, a "country devoted to the future," not forget the "values she cherished most." Islas characterizes the family as being "caught between the future and the past . . . some lived and died for the moment because they had to. The rest led double lives and followed the rules of both cultures as best they could" (42). The novel focuses on two who lead double lives, Josie, and her cousin, Miguel Chico. Both occupy a space outside of the Angel family: Josie for her rebellions against her mother's worldview, and especially her divorce, and Miguel Chico for his veiled writing about his family and his closeted homosexuality.

Josie is introduced first in the novel and occupies most of the narrative space of the book. Her mother, Eduvidges, like her grandmother, Mama Chona, raises her daughters to strictly follow the rules of their "Spanish" culture, and not to act on their "Indian" impulses. Josie has the greatest difficulty following her mother's decree. In her training, Mama Chona had, in fact, been successful with Eduvidges but not with two of her other daughters, Jesus Maria and Eufemia Maria. They, "Mama Chona knew, were two sides of the same coin—the spiritual and the sensual—and she predicted correctly that their lives would be filled with misery and heartache. Only Eduvidges seemed destined to enjoy some measure of worldly happiness" (37). Mama Chona had learned early in her life to scorn sentimental attachments and idealistic dreams. When the Mexican Revolution takes her oldest child, "Mama Chona wept for three days and three nights after he was in the ground and her children did not see her shed another tear for the rest of her life. 'Life is suffering,' she said to them. 'Life is letting go of what you love'" (41). Mama Chona's conviction is that suffering and injustice are endless and "that in a constant but always bloodless struggle for power, the God who spoke English with a Texas accent was almost always victorious and rewarded His minions with better paying jobs and more expensive homes in the nicer parts of town where the school are better." But she is also convinced that "the Catholic God of the migrants ordered His servants to multiply, and bided his time. Mama Chona vowed to wait by his side . . . Eduvidges waited along with her mother" (43). Mama Chona's spirituality is aware of the historical "facts" of being Chicano in Texas; she recognizes that injustice and suffering are manufactured by God "who spoke English," and that she is powerless before them. Catholicism is her way of making sense of what is around her, and it also gives her a sense of historical inevitability. What will come about, will come about—the key is to wait.

Mama Chona's favorite religious figure is Saint Therese of Lisieux, the Little Flower of Jesus, and she makes her the patron saint of the family. Mama Chona's daughters see the Carmelite saint as "what they were meant to be, and in the first years of their life in the desert, thinking about the Little Flower's physical suffering helped them put up with the stony conditions of their childhood and adolescence. Later, such early training led Mama Chona's daughters to be greatly disappointed in men." The granddaughters, including Josie, were told that "life in this human form was to be endured and that the only future that mattered was the after life . . . they were reminded that suffering was a given and as timeless as the desert around them" (46). Implicitly, if not explicitly, the women are being taught that to love is to suffer, to trust men is to be disappointed, and that the material world cannot provide any sort of lasting happiness. There is a merging of the "stony conditions" that they endured and the suffering they will undergo in the emotional realm. What Saint Therese symbolizes is a merging of physical and emotional anguish with ecstasy. In fact, in this ethos, suffering is not only historically inevitable, it can be transformed into the highest form of living.

Josie and Miguel Chico, however much they reject this medieval version of Catholic suffering and guilt, reinvent it on their own terms. While growing up, the two cousins create the "Order of Saint Wretched so that they might laugh at misery. Passion, betrayal, unrequited love were all offered up to Saint Wretched whenever the cousins found themselves or others once again enthralled by the sins of the flesh. Their favorite characters and writers were on the list of the suffering, and they spoke of them as living members of the Order" (57). This Order is introduced in the novel when Miguel Chico and Josie as teenagers go see a movie in which "the most beautiful woman in the world was dying in the arms of her lover, and Josie was struck by a fit of weeping . . . All she heard was the coughing that caused the woman on the screen to cling and bend in awful ways and still look gorgeous. In his panic, her lover, also gorgeous, yelled for the nurse. At last, he had realized the woman loved him and only him" (55). The two "gorgeous" actors are Greta Garbo and Robert Taylor, and the film is *Camille*, from 1937, by the gay director, George Cukor. (Hollywood historians such as Vito Russo have noted that none of these artists were known for their aggressive heterosexuality.)

In the midst of the death scene, Miguel Chico giggles, and Josie pinches him. While Josie thinks he has missed the beauty of the scene, "The truth was that he had been watching Josie because he had become infected by the woman's suffering. All tragedy affected him in that way. He could tolerate such pain for only so long before he had to breathe normally and remind himself to laugh or smile" (57). Miguel Chico feels suffocated and self-conscious of his responses. In the theater he is aware of other teenagers mocking the movie and doesn't want to expose himself in any way. His closetedness forces him to contain his emotions from the public at large, for fear of what might be revealed about him.

At a high school dance that Miguel Chico and Josie attend together, she meets her future husband in a typically theatrical way: "Another sheet of lightning lit up the room and was followed quickly by a long roll of thunder that signaled the end of the storm. The air in the room was heavy with the smell of greasewood and sage . . . Josie turned and saw the shadow of young man standing a few feet away from her. 'How melodramatic,' Josie said" (70). At this dance, Josie also takes notice of her cousin's behavior: "Her cousin bounced with ease with one group to another and was friendly to everyone, sometimes insincerely, Josie knew. His smile and wit opened doors that warned others to stay out. Though she envied his popularity and social grace, Josie thought her cousin one of the loneliest people in the world . . . Later that year, he was elected class favorite" (68). This high school dance is the last time that the cousins will be together before adulthood in the novel, and it is interesting that she formulates an appraisal of his character and meets her husband at this point. Miguel Chico's habit of ingratiating himself with people indeed keeps him very much alone, but Josie does not see, or better, does not mention, that the motivation behind this may be Miguel Chico's homosexuality, and his need to hide it to keep himself safe. At the risk of generalization, I don't think many gays and lesbians want to be remembered the way they were as adolescents, if they were forced (as many are) to be closeted about their identities. Often times homophobia is virulent enough to ensure that gay and lesbians are hardly given enough choices to even begin approximating what their real character will be like in the years to come. But I also don't want to suggest that since the scene is in the past, in the "repressive 1950s," that Miguel Chico was necessarily and prohibitively unable to reveal himself. The closet that he inhabits is not necessarily any less historically inflicted as he becomes an adult. Importantly, Josie is unable, or unwilling, to broach the differences between her and her cousin, contributing to each of their loneliness, especially after her return to Del Sapo years later after her divorce.

Christmas Misery

The novel's narrative center begins at a Christmas when Josie and Miguel Chico are both in Del Paso and both miserable. Miguel Chico is drinking a great deal, and Josie in turn is despondent over her husband leaving her and by her current lover, who she describes as drinking too much. The fact that it is Christmas only adds to the general misery. If Islas is concerned with representing the family as the site of Miguel Chico's alienation (and I think he is), the Catholic and Chicano family at Christmas only exacerbates this further. His intensely, if hypocritically, religious family will not allow exemption from their celebration for anyone, even when Miguel Chico is visibly dying of a broken heart. He is in the midst of spiritual and emotional suffering, not because he is gay (necessarily), but because he is unable to share, or imagine being able to share, his grief over a failed love to his stoically oblivious family. But in the context of his family, it is precisely this type of suffering that should be expected and endured with patience. So what Miguel Chico does is drink constantly throughout the holiday and mutter drunken inanities.

Miguel Chico and Josie share a moment, when Josie finally confesses her own unhappiness. Miguel Chico coaxes her to own up to her relationship troubles, "Are you sure you're still not getting down on your knees to Saint Wretched? I don't believe all this hysteria about Christmas

Eve is caused only by your mother and sister. Come on, cousin, confess. Where is the man in this picture of distraught, almost middle-aged womanhood?" Josie replies: "God, Mickie, you know I have more problems with men than you do . . . What's wrong with me? Tell me, Mickie. You know about men. Tell me." Miguel Chico does not answer. Instead, "he was looking away from her toward the silhouette of the mountain. In the silence that followed, Miguel Chico was embarrassed and felt ashamed. It was the first time she had stood in a non-joking way so near the gate of his secret territory. Years earlier and without having to be told, she had understood that her cousin was a lover of men. Their camaraderie as sinners was born out of that intuitive and unspoken revelation. When she became the only divorced woman in the family, they grew even closer and glowed in each other's company when sitting in the living rooms and dens of their relatives" (120).

Several assumptions are being made about Miguel Chico besides the basic fact of his, in the wonderfully florid fashion Islas excelled at, being a "lover of men." But why does Josie assume that Miguel Chico has problems with men? This information seems to have been conveyed to her intuitively, and unspoken, much like the fact of Miguel Chico's homosexuality. If their camaraderie as sinners brings them together, it is this very camaraderie that is being violated by being mentioned. Once the "open secret" was exposed, both of them are left feeling uncomfortable and ashamed. It bears exploring this embarrassment and shame assigned to Miguel Chico.

Eve Kosofsky Sedgwick, in *Epistemology of the Closet*, reads canonical U.S. and European texts by Melville, James, Wilde, Nietzsche, and Proust, as demonstrating a development from the end of the Nineteenth century that "left no space in the culture exempt from the potent incoherence of homo/heterosexual definition." Sedgwick notes that the readings "attend to performative aspects of texts . . . An assumption underlying the book is that the relations of the closet—the relations of the known and the unknown, the explicit and the inexplicit around homo/heterosexual definition—have the potential for being peculiarly revealing, in fact, about speech acts generally . . . But in the vicinity of the closet, even what counts as a speech act is problematized on a perfectly routine basis . . . 'Closetedness' itself is a performance initiated as such by the speech act of a silence—not a particular silence, but a silence that accrues particularity by fits and starts, in relation to the discourse that surrounds and differentially constitutes it" (3). To declare openly then, that one is now out of the closet does a particular kind of communicative work, just as not to ever say that one is gay performs another. It is then logical that to say—or to assume—that someone is gay—is also performative, producing narratives of identity formation, with or without consent. Sedgwick chooses an intriguing example to illustrate this point:

> The speech acts that coming out, in turn, can comprise are as strangely specific. And they have nothing to do with the acquisition of new information. I think of a man and a woman I know, best friends, who for years canvassed freely the emotional complications of each other's erotic lives—the man's eroticism happening to focus exclusively on men. But it was only after one particular conversational moment, fully a decade into this relationship, that it seemed to either of these friends that permission had been given to the woman to refer to the man, in their conversation together, as a gay man. Discussing it much later, both agreed they had felt at the time that one moment had constituted a clear-cut act of coming out, even in the context of years and years beforehand of exchange predicated on the man's being gay. What was said to make this difference? Not a version of "I am gay," which would have been bathetic between them. What constituted coming out for this man, in this situation, was to use about himself the phrase "coming out"—to mention, as if casually, having come out to someone else. (1990: 3–4)

I quote this passage at length because it so closely resembles Josie and Miguel Chico's interaction in the novel. Josie is clear that she had always known about Miguel Chico's gayness, and some allusion is made to their having joked about it before. But what is crucially different is that Josie does not have permission to refer to Miguel Chico as gay. When she makes her limp joke about it, it sounds like an insinuation, and she instantly regrets it. This exchange, too, takes place in the context of their relationship, and their family dynamics in history-laden Del Sapo.

In a certain sense, this scene can hardly qualify as "coming out" at all. In fact, Josie and Miguel Chico never again have this type of conversation; it doesn't open their relationship up to more "revealing" intimacies, or lead to any other revelations. Coming out narratives are typically about empowerment and a measure of pride. Here, instead, they are both left embarrassed by Josie's transgression. It is Miguel Chico who needs to do something, to act, to come out. When Josie attempts to do this for him, the dynamic is awkward and off-putting. Miguel Chico invokes Saint Wretched to Josie, and she thinks she can bring him to a discussion of why men have made them both suffer, but Miguel Chico cannot say a word. It is Miguel Chico's inability to worship at their altar of unrequited love, his drawing away from talking to Josie about his failed relationship that causes him more pain than his being in the closet about his homosexuality. It is his closetedness, his silence about his emotional life that doesn't let him transform his melancholia to something more useful, such as the campiness of Saint Wretched, which had served him well in the past. I do not want to suggest that if Miguel Chico would only just talk about it he would feel better. Instead, I mean to suggest that he and Josie had learned to performatively transform misery and grief through irony and wit, and now at a most crucial time, Miguel Chico seems to have forgotten how.

But it is this "talking about it" that is important also, since Josie herself feels perfectly comfortable flaunting her divorce and her misery. She knows "that what she was in the family's eyes was the sinner. Not one of her relatives—not even her mother—would have called her that to her face, for they were good Catholic people and needed mediation to guard them from truths and keep them comfortable. Instead some of the Angels let her know her place by shifting the atmosphere away from the tropical every time she, the fallen woman, arrived at a gathering of the tribe" (107). But though Josie may be a "fallen woman," she does not occupy the same "fallen" space Miguel Chico does. Miguel Chico may occupy a space closer to his Uncle Felix, who lived as married family man but was also a "lover of men."

The Pursuit of the Past

Uncle Felix's murder is only mentioned in *Migrant Souls* immediately after Josie's question to Miguel Chico. It hovers like one more ghost in the family; a murder that was bloody and senseless, and yet was not enough to effectively lift the curtain of denial that plagued the family. In *The Rain God* the murder takes up an entire chapter, in which Felix is described as being a foreman, who conducts his own intimate medical examinations of the illegal labor he hires. The workers are indulgent of him, because of his good nature (*Rain God* 115–116). Felix also hangs out in a bar near his work where underage serviceman stationed in Del Sapo congregate. One fateful, terrible day Felix is at the bar drinking a beer, morose over a fight with his favorite child JoEl, and listening to an "old romantic Mexican ballad . . . playing on the jukebox . . . As usual the singer was suffering from love and Felix smiled at the sentimentality of the lyrics . . . To himself he thought how only a Mexican song could mix sadness and laughter like that so that one could cry and sing at the same time" (126). Felix begins talking with a soldier who claims he is twenty-one. Felix notices his mouth and muses how, "he had long since stopped wondering why his pursuit of the past led him to young men instead of women. He was secure in the love of his children, even when they quarreled with him, and he knew that Angie loved him. He was not looking for any of them in this boy's mouth. He was looking for something else" (135). Felix offers to drive him back to the base, but stops at a canyon, where the soldier beats him to death after Felix makes advances on him.

This murder is recounted and remembered in the moment after Miguel Chico's desire is named by someone else. Eduvidges' proclamation after the newspaper reveals Felix's hidden life, "I don't believe a word of it. There are no homosexuals," infuriates Josie. She sees the hypocrisy, not only the family engages in, but the State, represented by Felix's father, who does not press a further investigation because of family shame. Miguel Chico's own reaction to Felix's death is not recorded in the narrative, but is instead allowed to permeate— unspoken—through his identity. Uncle Felix becomes a symbol not only of lies, but the violence that is perpetuated, and even allowed, as long as these lies are not disturbed. This is, perhaps, Islas' strongest, most literal condemnation. Felix seems to represent the fate of a sexuality that is not allowed expression—which is not allowed to live—in Del Sapo. In this sense, Miguel Chico represents the other fate, as he walks through the family holidays as the drunken embodiment of sorrow.

It is on the subsequent Christmas Eve that we finally hear the story of Miguel Chico's heartbreak. Josie and he take her daughters out to a bar before they go to the annual dinner at a relative's. Miguel Chico goes to the bathroom and there facing the mirror he remembers:

> Once, against all laws of nature, snow had fallen in the Bay Area. Miguel Chico and Sam Godwin walked through the streets . . . in the early morning before any traffic sullied the whiteness of the world . . . They had shared a flat on Guerrero Street in San Francisco for three years. When Sam left California to be a corporate accountant in New York City, Miguel Chico felt the world had ended. Six months later, hanging on to a shrunken sink in Del Sapo, Texas, he was still in mourning as only an Angel can mourn. Passion had led him to believe that the Sam he loved had been real. (208)

While the story is fairly straightforward, Islas uses the snow imagery to suggest that nothing was "real" about the relationship, that it was "against all the laws of nature" that it even happened. But there is no ambiguity that this is a relationship between two men, and that it caused him real pain, not only because it ended, but also because of his own belief in the "realness" of his passion and his lover. Saint Wretched had led him astray.

The story, though, is told to no one, except the reader. It's as if Islas/Miguel Chico is unable to come out to Josie, or the family, but in the guise of an author, he can reveal "fictional" truths. This is precisely what he is accused of when he returns to the table and Josie says to him, "You have to stop writing about our perfectly happy family ... The older generation does not approve. They think you're telling their terrible secrets to the world and they don't like it ... I keep telling them all it's fiction and they keep wanting to believe every word" (210). It makes one wonder whether they noticed the person telling the story is obliquely revealing his own "terrible secrets." It is on this Christmas that Miguel Chico feels like a failure, that he must destroy himself, that nothing he has ever done, or can do, will defeat the world that he came from, and in which he lives.

Islas's novels contain as their themes memory, history, and writing itself. But what haunts them is the closet that the narrator inhabits, and this represents the larger thematic concern—form. The very form of *Migrant Souls* is a closet—in the sense that is cannot reveal the "real" town it describes. It changes names, it clouds events, and its time structure is complex, if not convoluted. But what keeps it from being a coy exercise in autobiography is the symbol of Saint Wretched. This symbol of suffering, of unrequited love, of unhappiness itself, is championed in the book because it is a recognition of how the people in Del Sapo actually live and make sense of their lives. The condition of suffering is what Grossberg describes as an "affective investment," which "in certain practices always returns some interest through a variety of empowering relations: by producing further energy ... by placing people in a position from which they feel they have a certain control over their (affective) life; or by reaffirming the feeling that one is still alive and that this matters. In all of these cases, affective empowerment enables one to go on, to continue to struggle to make a difference. The investment in popular practices opens up strategies which enable one to invest in new forms of meaning, pleasure and identity, and to cope with new forms of pain, pessimism, frustration, alienation, terror and boredom" (85–86).

But this is not to say that the point of the novel is that people are generally miserable. It is to suggest that finding misery in passion, that finding despair in hope, are precisely the tools of political autobiography and history. The narrative production of *Migrant Souls* in a sense depends on unrequited love and on romantic unhappiness, but this paradoxically, makes it no less a celebration of them. Importantly, the real material conditions of the borderlands of the Southwest are opaquely, but definitively, drawn in the novels, and are held responsible for this unhappiness. If homosexuality figures in the novel as a host of repression and guilt, it is also the site of great energy and production, leading to violence and despair, surely, but also to the greatest emotional heights that the gay characters can reach. When race and sexuality are considered, concepts such as the closet become even less transparent. To come out of the closet, when one is also marked by race, highlights the shaky *and* liberatory promises that coming out makes. The Chicano closet in Islas' texts becomes a literary trope that combats homophobic cultural expectations by the existence and presence of a counter-narrative. It combats them because it can transform the culture that represses it. It defeats the closet because it draws from the very culture and materials that deny it full expression: it is repression that creates the Chicano Closet.

Chapter 3
Utopian Drag and Gender Politics

In a discussion that critically assesses gay male expressive culture (such as camp and melodramatic romance), it should not seem surprising to introduce the question of drag. If queer theory has ascended in contemporary academic theoretical venues as the singular approach to gay/lesbian studies, then drag can be considered central to queer theory itself. Drag embodies many important, conflicted questions about contemporary urban queer identities and gay male identities in particular. In fact, the drag queen can represent a vital fixture in a gay pride parade or a homophobic representation in mass culture. Here are some assumptions about drag that function as queer common sense:

(a) The almost total conflation of effeminacy and female identification with gay male identity. This assumption comes from homophobic versions of psychoanalytic theories of sexual development, along with general assumptions of gay male psychology. This assumption circulates around the noxious notion of a gay man being in fact a type of "woman" who desires a "man." In vulgar Freudian terms, this is the invert theory of sexuality.
(b) The historical centrality of drag practice to gay identity. This is best symbolized by Stonewall, in which, gay historical mythology relates, it was drag queens who began the Gay Liberation Movement. This assumption rests on the idea of drag queens as not just resistant to bourgeois norms of gender and social propriety, but as being braver and more militant than "typical" gay men.
(c) The spectacle of drag and its associations with glamour and "fabulousness." Not only feeding into popular ideas of gay men as being somehow more in tune with fashion and taste, the drag queen symbolizes the consumerist extravagance, if not wastefulness, of the gay male community.
(d) Drag as comedy and as embodying the gay practice of camp and irony. Camp refuses to take anything seriously, and the drag

queen is given comic license to joke about anything, from the morbid to the racially insensitive. The drag queen can also make an absurdity of the costume itself and appear in drag with a beard, or sloppily applied make-up.

(e) The pathos of drag and its associations with excessive emotion and sentiment. This is the drag queen who assumes the melodramatic pose, investing each emotion with great significance. This drag queen also relies upon sincerity tinged with irony, no small achievement.

(f) And for our purposes, I would like to suggest the importance of drag to black and Latino gay cultures. Drag often foregrounds the particular cultural significance of gender to these communities. Drag may occupy an important space in racially marked gay men, and perhaps this is because of the particular historical formations of masculinity and femininity in these communities.

What these assumptions share in common, besides their varying degree of circulation, is that they involve notions of performance. It is difficult to conceive of drag as not consisting of a type of stage activity and of being a part of a theatrical spectacular. I begin my discussion by situating drag's importance to queer theory by considering anthropologist Esther Newton's book, *Mother Camp: Female Impersonators in America*. In framing drag's importance to queer theory, it is vital to consider drag practice also as a particular expression of racial identity. Moving through critical responses to the 1990 film *Paris Is Burning*, I theorize the problem of drag and fantasy—fantasies about stardom and glamor, fantasies about wealth and romantic love, and fantasies about one's own identity. These fantasies are contemplated within the context in which they are produced: in the bodies and minds of queer people of color. Drag's relationship to sexual and racial identities is discussed in a context in which relatively visible academic work about drag, such as Marjorie Garber's *Vested Interests: Cross Dressing and Cultural Anxiety*, often elides these concerns. Through *Paris is Burning*, I consider drag as emblematic of unrequited love and dreams of utopia. This is drag as pathos; drag as *Hollywood* pathos is perhaps the most compelling consideration, as in the example of Judy Garland and her impersonators. The "suffering woman" occupies much of my thought about gay men of color and their relationship to the world at large. This provides a useful segue to my discussion of Manuel Puig's *Kiss of the Spider Woman* in the next chapter.

But What is Drag? The Problem of Specificity

In this discussion, I focus on drag as a cultural expression by gay men which takes place in a performance space of some type, often a bar or club. That my definition can be read mundanely belies the rich and contested territory of drag and gender studies. Often when reading various theoretical and sociological accounts of drag practice, one becomes confused by what particular definition of drag is being used. For example, drag can become another fulsome signifier, in which varied and historically specific meanings become deflated and conflated. While not wanting to impose limits upon the meanings and potential practices that drag signifies, I would like in this discussion, to be clear about what type of drag performance I am critiquing, and what types of political gestures that performance could be making. At this point, I am not specifically referring to the political intentions of various theorists of drag, but instead I am emphasizing how important *specificity* is in analyzing any cultural production or representation.

Like any other representation, drag has been called upon to serve various contested meanings, which can often become confused and contradictory. But what makes drag particularly useful for study is its rich connections to theatrical display and sexual identity; it can create a charge—both intellectual and erotic—for its audiences. This charge can also provoke hostile reactions aimed not only at such ostentatious displays, but at the irreverence that drag performs toward gender and other identities.

In so many ways, drag is central to gay culture (if not synonymous with it) precisely because drag is the most visible definition of gay male camp. As Esther Newton points out in her study, *Mother Camp: Female Impersonators in America*, "The ubiquity of the camp style and role in most homosexual groups, regardless of the status position of the group, is one of the most striking features of homosexual culture. As camp style represents all that is most unique in the homosexual subculture, the camp is the cultural and social focus of the majority of male homosexual groups" (56). Camp is notoriously difficult to define, but Newton offers this explanation: "Camp is not a thing. More broadly it signifies a relationship between things, people, and activities or qualities, with homosexuality. In this sense, 'camp taste,' for instance, is synonymous with homosexual taste... camp is in the eye of the beholder... but it is assumed that there is an underlying unity of perspective among homosexuals: incongruity, theatricality, and humor" (105).

As an example of incongruity, Newton describes "masculine–feminine juxtapositions" as the most characteristic kind of camp. This would include an intensely masculine man in full drag, or as one of Newton's informants offers, "the basic homosexual experience . . . Camp is all based on homosexual thought. It is all based on the idea of two men or two women in bed. It's incongruous and it's funny." This incongruity becomes a perspective on everyday life; it includes "juxtapositions of high and low status, youth and old age, profane and sacred functions or symbols, cheap and expensive articles." This relationship between persons and/or objects that inhabit very different social locations is what can create camp; "Camp inheres not in the person or thing itself but in the tension between that person or thing and the context or association" (107). The exciting analytic relationship Newton makes between camp and gay identity itself makes clear the function of camp in organizing a sensibility.

The next feature—theatricality—Newton describes as operating in "three interlocking ways . . . camp is style. Importance tends to shift from what a thing is to how it looks, and what is done to how it is done . . . camp is also exaggerated, consciously 'stagy,' specifically theatrical . . . The second aspect of theatricality in camp is its dramatic form. Camp, like drag, always involves a performer or performers and an audience. This is its structure." The third point Newton makes about its theatricality is "camp is suffused with the perception of 'being as playing a role' and 'life as theatre.' It is at this point that drag and camp merge and augment each other" (107). This theatricality can operate in specific ways, as being the particular role that a gay person would have to play in a homophobic world—and the consciousness of playing this role that a gay person would have. In this sense, being in the closet becomes not only a specific "theatrical" role, it becomes a contradiction in terms: to be in the closet requires that one be gay in the first place. In other ways, this theatricality becomes part of how gay men socialize—how the social interaction between them creates an awareness of the artificiality of gender roles and sexual mores in general. Gay people know (if they know themselves at all) that all is not as it seems. As Newton describes, "At the informal level, a great deal of 'camping' goes on wherever gay people congregate at parties, bars, and beaches, in which female identification of one sort of another is a large component. This is equivalent to saying that homosexual gatherings do not discourage, and frequently encourage, by means of an appreciative audience, the expression of this identification" (34). Along with the importance of camp's relationship to female identification for gay men, the theatrical aspect of camp requires an audience. This, in turn, can create the prospect for community, or communally shared meanings and codes.

The last quality of camp Newton describes is its humor. "Camp is for fun; the aim of camp is to make an audience laugh. In fact, it is a system of humor" (34). This may be its most accessible (although at the same time its most baffling and misunderstood) characteristic for those outside of camp's historical meanings. The comic drag queen, the ridiculous femmy man, the fussy queen: all of these are familiar stereotypes in popular culture, especially films and television. But Newton makes the point that "Camp humor is a system of laughing at one's incongruous position instead of crying. That is, the humor does not cover up, it transforms. I saw the reverse transformation—from laughter to pathos—often enough, and it is axiomatic for the impersonators that when the camp cannot laugh, he dissolves into a maudlin bundle of self-pity" (109). This "maudlin bundle" is what compels my interest. If camp is made up of incongruity, theatricality, and humor, I would argue this relates precisely to its maudlin self-pity and melancholic sense of loss. Interestingly, Newton reached these conclusions not only through her fieldwork, which I discuss more in detail below, but also by observing gay men's emotional connections with Hollywood movies.

Mother of Camp

Mother Camp, began as Newton's doctoral dissertation in anthropology, which she completed in 1968; the book was published in 1972. From about 1965 to 1968, Newton did field work in Chicago and Kansas City, interviewing and attending nightly drag shows. While in many ways, she describes a gay community on the threshold of Stonewall, her observations, as she herself remarks in a later introduction, "strikes me still as an accurate analysis of its subject: drag queens as gay male culture 'heroes' in the mid-sixties." Newton describes her work, especially the book, as having been shaped by a framework that includes "the Viet Nam war, the rise of Black, Feminist, and Gay consciousness and the collapse of legitimacy in American institutions (including universities)." It was, Newton explains, "Women's Liberation particularly [which] led me to experience the arbitrariness of our sex roles. I know now (rather than think) that the structure of sex roles is maintained by the acquiescence of all the participants who accept their fate as natural and legitimate" (xvi). These concerns, at least, those of sex and gender roles and their instability, of course remain hotly contested terms in feminist and queer theory. That Newton in a sense formulated these observations about gender through drag queens is prescient, as we shall see.

While Newton effectively argues for the connection between gay male identity and drag, if not for gay male identity and camp, she also describes drag as being such "an effective symbol of both the outside-inside and masculine-feminine oppositions." Through this, she works out a theory of gender construction:

> At the simplest level, drag signifies that the person wearing it is a homosexual, that he is a male who is behaving in a specifically inappropriate way, that he is a male who places himself as a woman in relation to other men . . . At the most complex, it is a double inversion that says "appearance is an illusion." Drag says, "my outside appearance is feminine, but my essence 'inside' is masculine." At the same time it symbolizes the opposite inversion: "my appearance 'outside' is masculine but my essence 'inside' is feminine." (103)

What Newton is pointing out is that drag can foreground not only the illusion of (gender) appearances, but that this illusion does not operate in a strict binary: the opposite of illusion is not necessarily reality. The drag queen reflects back and forth various gender "truths."

One of Newton's most important insights about drag is that the "effect of the drag system is to wrench the sex roles loose from that which supposedly determines them, that is, genital sex. Gay people know sex-typed behavior can be achieved, contrary to what is popularly believed. They know that the possession of one type of genital equipment by no means guarantees the 'naturally appropriate' behavior" (103). The disconnection made by drag between sex roles and genitals opens up a new vista for considering gender and sexuality. The drag queen, through incongruity, theatricality, and humor, not only collapses societal expectations, but also operates as a banner of some type for gay identity itself. As Newton describes it, "The impersonator, like the camp, is flaunting his homosexuality on a stage, without any apology. Not all gay people want to wear drag, but drag symbolizes gayness. The drag queen symbolizes an open declaration, even celebration, of homosexuality" (64).

While I do not have any problem with championing the drag queen as an "open declaration" of male homosexuality, I would want to be careful of romanticizing too fully any type of cultural practice. This is not just because romanticization can often obscure more ambiguous meanings in any cultural text, but also because it is still not entirely clear which type of specific drag queen is under investigation. What is clear is that the drag queen in the most general sense strikes quite forcefully at notions of gender identity. What I argue then, besides the importance of drag and camp to gay male identity, is how important the concept of gender and its construction has been not only for queer theory but also for the production of various queer affirmative practices and readings. Importantly, gender construction as such, comes to be (perfectly, if not problematically) exemplified through the drag queen and drag practice. But what exactly gets opened up by destabilizing gender, especially in queer projects?

Garber and the "Universalism" of Drag

As noted earlier, in contemporary theoretical formulations of drag, there is often little historical specificity about exactly what kind of drag is being discussed. In *Mother Camp*, Newton distinguishes at least two types of drag queens: the "street impersonator" and the "stage impersonator." The street impersonator is described as a "fusion of the 'street fairy' life with the profession of female impersonation." Street fairies are described as "jobless young homosexual men who publicly epitomize the homosexual stereotype and are the underclass of the gay world . . . Street impersonators are never off stage . . . their way of life is collective, illegal, and immediate . . . its central experiences are confrontation prostitution, and drug 'highs.' " The stage impersonator, on the other hand, makes a clear distinction between public and private life. Performing on stage is "work . . . viewed as a profession with goals and standards . . . stage impersonators are 'individualistic,' relatively 'respectable' " (8).

Newton emphasized that "nothing is more characteristic of the street impersonator than his public presentation of himself. Street fairies specialize in public, confrontation deviance. While respectable homosexuals and stage impersonators attempt to 'pass' or at least draw a minimum of attention to themselves in public situations, street impersonators make themselves conspicuous" (8). This, I think, is a crucial distinction between the groups, and one that situates their respective political and social aims quite differently. Both groups consist of drag queens, therefore both groups are organized around the idea of gender play and impersonation, but there is a clear material difference of privilege and spectacle between the two groups. Although both groups are marginalized by their homosexuality, they occupy very different social and economic spaces, with very different motivations.

Street fairies often live in groups together; their living spaces, Newton emphasizes, "are not 'homes.' They are places to come in off the street, places to 'hole up' during the day. 'Husbands,' 'tricks,' and numerous acquaintances from the street life come in and out constantly. Any friend who needs a place to rest, recover from a 'high,' or get a new one, can generally 'fall by' and stay for a couple of hours or a couple of weeks" (12). Stage impersonators, on the other hand, compartmentalize their lives, and "tend to live farther away from clubs than street impersonators . . . in this, as in much else, stage impersonators act on basically middle-class conceptions of appropriate living arrangements" (17). The street impersonators live their lives completely out of every type of mainstream. They "literally live outside the law, in the use of assault, in the distribution and consumption of drugs, in the nature of their sexual activities including the sale of sex, and often in their very physical appearance" (14). The street fairy does not have any investment whatsoever in what Newton describes as "straight" society: "from their perspective, all of respectable society seems square, distant and hypocritical" (15). This attitude corresponds to their drag performances. Newton notes how they view "the work instrumentally, that is, as a way of making money to live." For this reason they often lip synch, mouthing the words to songs from records, as opposed to the stage impersonators' use of their own voices and reliance on personal talents and abilities. While the professional stage impersonator wants to bring the audience in, and to develop a rapport, to present a sophisticated, if campy, ambiance throughout a performance, the street impersonator does an act bordering on surly. As Newton describes it: "On the stage, the street impersonators are sometimes openly contemptuous of the audience. They tend to perform as if the stage were a dramatic encapsulation of the street confrontations with the public . . . they are often wrapped in a trance-like state, never looking at the audience and simply going through their routines" (11–12).

Conversely, the stage impersonators constantly stress professionalism, and often "express nothing but contempt for queens who refuse to segregate their activities into clearly defined work and private domains" (17). Of course, the clear distinction between the public and private realms, or being able to have a clear distinction between the two, is important for the maintenance of the bourgeoisie. At this point, Newton describes an interview she had with a professional stage impersonator, which is important to quote in full for the clear distinctions that are made by the subject himself:

Esther Newton: Why, by the way, don't you like "drag queen"? You prefer the term "female impersonator"?
Informant: To me I think "drag queen" is sort of like a street fairy puttin' a dress on. Tryin' to impress somebody, but "female impersonator" sounds more professional.

EN:	What about . . . let's start from scratch. What is a 'street fairy'?
I:	It's a little painted queen that wants to run around with make-up on in the street and have long hair, and everything, to draw attention . . .
EN:	I want you to make a distinction between street fairies and people who are professional. What's the difference?
I:	Well, in the first place, when I put my make-up on, I am putting it on for a reason. I never wear make-up out on the street, because I don't think anyone needs a neon sign telling what they are! These little street fairies evidently can't get enough attention, so they use this make-up, pile their hair up, and all this, just to draw attention. (His tone is vehement, contemptuous.) I have my attention when I'm on stage; they have to have it by looking absolutely ridiculous. (17)

Which is the more oppositional? Which is challenging gender norms in a more productive manner? The street impersonator's ability to have wide spread cultural and social effects seems limited by his marginality, even from the gay community. The stage impersonator is limited by compliance with bourgeois norms of respectability and conventionality. The stage impersonator quoted above is described as being "vehement" about the spectacle of the street fairies. Indeed, even someone participating in disrupting gender on a stage shares this discomfort with the "outer edges" of gay identity. While neither one seems to occupy a position of "seamless oppositionality," Newton does note that she "was not surprised to see that the first collective homosexual revolt in history, the 'battle of the Stonewall' . . . was instigated by street fairies. Street fairies have nothing to lose" (18–19). In this particular case, it was those with "nothing to lose" who were able to make the political connections between their public and private lives, and make a crucial decision to rebel, to fight back, and to ultimately ignite the political struggle of gays and lesbians in the United States. But what of the stage impersonators? I am uncomfortable with giving them an apolitical role in the struggle, or worse, a reactionary one. In fact, I would argue that the force and visibility of stage impersonators in the gay community before and after Stonewall attest to the representational importance of theatrical display and gender identity in the community itself. There are important differences between these two groups of drag performers, which contribute not only to the difference in their aims, but also in their effects.

It is crucial differences such as these that are absent in Marjorie Garber's popular (for an academic work) *Vested Interests: Cross-Dressing and Cultural Anxiety*. In this wonderfully written book, Garber traverses through Western Culture for examples of what she calls "the transvestite figure." Through readings of Shakespeare, Hollywood movies such as *Tootsie*, and the fantasies of Lawrence of Arabia (to take just three examples), Garber wants to argue that:

> The binarism male/female, one apparent ground of distinction, is itself put in question or under erasure in transvestitism, and a transvestite figure, or a transvestite mode, will always function as a site of overdetermination—a mechanism of displacement from one blurred boundary to another... What this book insists upon... is that transvestitism is a space of possibility structuring and confounding culture: The disruptive elements that intervenes, not just a category crisis of male and female, but the crisis of category itself. (17)

This is an intriguing and ambitious thesis, and Garber indeed takes the reader along a sweeping journey through various representations; but exactly what Garber is talking and making claims about remains a serious problem for me. By Garber's generalized and nonspecific use of "transvestite" to describe what it is that cross-dressers, fetishists, drag queens, straight drag, transsexuals, Shakespearean boy-actors, Gertrude Stein, Milton Berle, Annie Lennox, Liberace, and Elvis (to name a few) actually *do*, seems imprecise and ineffectual. Besides the connotations of "transvestite," which imply a sexologist classification of a man's sexual fetish for wearing women's clothes, Garber's casual use of the term to describe both real people and cultural texts seems irresponsible and culturally insensitive.

Vested Interests is, oddly, not a very gay book. In what feels like a perfunctory chapter entitled, "Breaking the Code: Transvestitism and Gay Identity," Garber raises a key question, "In a homophobic and norm-obsessed culture then, does 'transvestite' really after all become a code word for 'gay and lesbian'?" (131). In this chapter at least, "transvestite" refers to "drag queen." The chapter begins with Garber citing television talk shows, such as *Geraldo* and *Donahue* in which straight men claim that their cross-dressing in women's clothing has nothing to do with their heterosexuality. Garber goes on to make the point that the audiences seem skeptical about this claim, and comments that the "conflation of transvestitism and gay identity has become a political factor for both of the populations most directly concerned" (131). This type of opposition is indeed an intriguing one, a battle between competing groups for control of the sign of clothing, and what it can "mean" about gender and sexuality. But the problem may be even more vexed than Garber allows.

Drag Makes Its Point

If cross-dressing can mean entirely different things to straight male transvestites and to gay drag queens, I argue that at least in the case of gay drag queens, cross-dressing itself has several competing meanings even within gay expressive culture. Garber gets at this problem: "The politics of drag are complicated by persistent divisions within gay male culture about the relationship of 'dressing up' to gay male identity. Is the drag queen a misogynist put-down of women, a self-hating parody, or a complex cultural sign that defies any simple translation into 'meaning'?" (149). In fact, I think that the drag queen in gay culture can be all of those things. I also believe, along with Newton, that the drag queen functions as a type of representation of gay male identity itself. What is crucial to this understanding is to underscore that like any other identity and representation, it remains a ground of contestation, contradiction, and profound ambiguity. This is precisely what gives the drag queen such potency as a cultural symbol. In fact, there is finally not "the" drag queen, but instead a plurality of drag queens with proliferating meanings and possibilities and histories. This point is important because I am not convinced that Garber grasps (or perhaps is even interested in) how and why drag queens can matter so much to gay people.

This is not to say that all gay people have a natural affinity for drag queens, or that all gay people take pleasure in, or even give credit to drag queens for their performance or their politics. But I argue that (in Grossberg's terms), drag queen performances are sites in which "affective investments" can be made. A drag queen performance can provoke, or at least comment upon, various emotional and cultural aspirations on the part of gay people. Particular, but not all, drag performances, in their expressive use of narratives of stardom, glamour, and heartbreak, can speak to gay men in their aspirations for "something better than this." This utopian urge, bound up so tightly with consumer capitalism and Hollywood-manufactured dreams, compels particular drag performances to express fantasies that cannot be merely reduced to masochism or commodification. They are instead, historically inflected responses to particular material conditions. But that is not all they are, and here I would like to look at two types of drag performances as examples.

My first case study is that of Judy Garland. Through the work of Richard Dyer, I describe the importance of "intensity of feeling" to drag, along with the image of the "star." The drag I am describing here relies upon the outer trappings of glitter and the inner trappings of suffering to do its work. Then I discuss the case of *Paris is Burning*, especially to think about what it means for these aspirations of glamor and fame to be racially inflected. When drag performance becomes about gender and race, its utopian longings become, I argue, not only more poignant, but more affectively effective.

Stardom, Drag, and Heartache: The Case of Judy Garland

There is a certainty about the link between gay male identity and the iconic figure of Judy Garland. While it seems like a quaint cliché to talk about the devotion of gay men toward Judy, this quaintness may come from a suspicion that her importance to gay culture has waned in the years since her historic 1962 Carnegie Hall concert. But if it is waning, it will probably continue to wane for many more years. Still, "Judy Garland" as a representation may have become somewhat of an embarrassment for gay men, a hysterical reminder of the dark days before Stonewall, when loving Judy functioned not only as a code for other gays ("Friends of Judy"), but also when the kind of pathos that Judy represented through her life and music seemed the most apt description of life in the closet. The "contemporary" (a most imprecise historical designation) gay man has little need for such relics of self-abuse and grandiloquent suffering. But I argue that Judy Garland remains an important representation in gay male self-styling especially, but not exclusively, through drag performance. I also want to suggest that the particular emotional stylization of Judy and her music still contains important resources for gay men to "make sense" of their emotional lives, by providing a historical and cultural context in which to consider them. In this sense, camp provides not only a sense of history, and a sense of irony, but also a tool for survival.

In his seminal book, *Heavenly Bodies: Film Stars and Society*, Richard Dyer includes a chapter entitled, "Judy Garland and Gay Men," in which he explores "how specific aspects of Garland's image could make a particular set of sense for gay men" (142). The question Dyer formulates hinges upon this: "Why the special felt affinity between this 'emotional' star and this oppressed group?" (153). Dyer describes how after about 1950, Judy Garland's image as a public star began taking on a radically different perspective from her image as the "girl next door," and that this led to her increasing significance to gay culture. I would like to begin with considering Judy Garland in her most representative film role in *The Wizard of Oz*, and her last film for Hollywood, *A Star is Born*.

Judy Garland was born in 1922, and began performing on the vaudeville stage at age three. She became a huge star by poignantly singing "Dear Mr. Gable" to a photograph of Clark Gable, in MGM's *Broadway*

Melody of 1938. The following year, she played little Dorothy Gale from Kansas in the musical film, *The Wizard of Oz.* Only seventeen at the time, this is the role for which she is most widely known. Garland played Dorothy with a combination of wide-eyed naiveté and sophisticated gumption, which could probably only have come from her extensive background in show business. Her performance, though, is of course characterized by her singing of "Over the Rainbow." Composed by Harold Arlen and E. Y. Harburg for the film, this song will forever be associated with Garland, with female impersonators "doing Judy," and even with gay urban culture itself with its insistent rainbow decor.

The song occurs rather early in the film, when Judy and Toto are still in Kansas, and everything is in black and white. The glorious MGM color is a cyclone away, and Dorothy/Judy has been told to find somewhere "where there isn't any trouble." Singing by herself, with only Toto as company, she muses:

> Somewhere, over the rainbow,
> Way up high;
> There's a land that I heard of once,
> In a lullaby.
> Somewhere, over the rainbow,
> Skies are blue,
> And the dreams that you dare to dream
> Really do come true.
> Someday I'll wish upon a star
> And wake up where the clouds are far behind me.
> Where troubles melt like lemon drops
> Away above the chimney tops,
> That's where you'll find me.
> Somewhere over the rainbow,
> Bluebirds fly—Birds fly over the rainbow,
> Why then, oh why then, can't I?
> If happy little bluebirds fly beyond the rainbow,
> Why, oh why, can't I?

The plaintiveness of the song is reflected in its ending with a question, a question that doesn't have an answer, since it is based on an impossibility: "over the rainbow" doesn't really exist. In the film itself, Dorothy is longing for a place that is less dreary and oppressive than Kansas. Meaningfully, the song is filled with fantasy imagery, words of the imagination, but this is hardly a children's song. Its passionate sense of longing crosses into very adult aspirations. If the song "makes sense" in the fantasy film—Dorothy does indeed end up "over the rainbow" in

Oz—it also makes sense to consider why this particular song became so associated with Judy Garland, and by default, with gay men. One explanation for the mournfulness of the song comes from the unchildlike voice that sings it. There is a sophisticated knowingness about the delivery, a sense that the singer truly is desperately yearning to go somewhere "over the rainbow." This is a song about reaching for, longing for somewhere else, which sounds very sad. This is an irony worthy of the richest type of camp expression, that a childlike song, with fantasy imagery in a fantasy film, could contain both utopian yearning (Where all the dreams you dream really do come true) and heartbreaking despair ("Why, oh why, can't I?"). It's not a stretch to read Oz as a place yearned for by gay people living in oppressive environments. Oz is in vivid color, where the imagination is valued and even necessary. "Over the Rainbow" then becomes a queer anthem expressing a longing for a place of acceptance and pleasure. The song, along with the entire movie, also operates in another way, showing the possibility of utopias in general (which is also applicable to a gay reading).

Importantly, Garland's performance of the song (both in the movie, and subsequently, in concerts) does inject a tone of great sadness, a sadness not just that this utopia does not exist, but that perhaps any utopia comes with a price—the giving up completely of the conditions that created the longing for a utopia in the first place. In the film, Dorothy becomes desperately homesick, and returns home by repeating, "There's no place like home." The contradiction that she would want to leave the wonderful land of Oz to return to colorless Kansas may come about because of the nature of these types of utopias created by show business and Hollywood. The movie seems to want the spectator to equate Oz with the magical possibilities of Hollywood. But there is often a built-in sense of dissatisfaction with "dreams coming true" in many Hollywood narratives: the talented person who climbs her way to the top, only to find it empty and meaningless, without any of the "sincerity" that comes from prosaic, everyday life. Garland's heartbreak in the song may come from her own awareness that the dream of Hollywood is a sham, filled with commodified depersonalization and the primacy of profit over talent and vision. But it also comes from the love of that type of dream—which she cannot let go of. If we long to go "over the rainbow," we are caught in a double bind of sorts; the very powerful feelings that create a longing for a utopia without homophobia or exploitation or racism are the ones that would cease to exist in that utopia.

In 1950, Garland was fired from MGM because of her erratic behavior, probably due to amphetamine abuse and depression, and later in the year, she attempted suicide. She subsequently began her first in a series of comebacks, reappearing on the stage or the screen triumphant until the next setback. Dyer describes the "comeback" as the "defining motif of the register of feeling" he characterizes in Garland. He describes it as "always having come back from something (sufferings and tribulations) and always keep on coming, no matter what" (151). With her increasing troubles, Garland began to assume a reputation for suffering—and surviving. This was reflected in her performances, which, as Dyer points out, always referred to:

> ... the emotional quality ... the immediate vivid intense experience of it ... The kind of emotion Garland expressed is somewhat differently described in the gay writings, but on two points all agree—that it is always strong emotion, and that it is really felt by the star herself and shared with the audience ... Although these are qualities that might be attributed to many stars, it is the particular register of intense, authentic feeling that is important here, a combination of strength and suffering and precisely the one in the fact of the other. Wherever the emphasis comes it is always the one in relation to the other, the strength inspirational because of the pressure of suffering behind it, the suffering keen because it has been stood up to so bravely. (149–150)

Judy indeed kept coming back, and in 1954, she registered her greatest triumph on screen since her role as Dorothy. She starred as Esther Blodgett in *A Star is Born*, directed by George Cukor. Garland was nominated for a Best Actress Oscar for her role as an up and coming actress who meets and falls in love with a star, Norman Maine (played by James Mason), on his alcoholic way down. The movie has a classic melodramatic plot, as it hinges on the woman giving up her career for the sake of her self-destructive man. He, discovering her sacrifice, commits suicide. The story had been filmed twice before, with Janet Gaynor and Fredric March in 1937, directed by William Wellman (same title), and as *What Price Hollywood?* in 1932, with Constance Bennett, directed by George Cukor. The different versions of the movie all hinge upon the heavy price paid for Hollywood stardom, but the version with Garland was the first to include music.

Judy, in the film, is discovered by James Mason singing after-hours in a jazz nightclub. Mason stumbles in and hears Judy singing:

> The night is bitter, the stars have lost their glitter
> The winds grow colder, and suddenly you're older,
> And all because of the Man That Got Away;
> No more his eager call, the writings on the wall,

> The dreams you dreamed have all gone astray.
> The man that won you, has run off and undone you,
> That great beginning has seen a final inning.
> Don't know what happened, it's all a crazy game;
> No more that all time thrill, for you've been through the mill.
> And never a new love will be the same.
> Good riddance, goodbye; every trick of his, you're onto,
> But fools will be fools, and where's he gone to?
> The road gets rougher, it's lonelier and tougher
> The hope you burn up, Tomorrow he might turn up,
> There's just no let up, the live long night and day,
> Ever since this world began, There is nothing sadder than,
> The one man, woman, looking for
> The Man That Got Away.

And stunningly, a star is born. Not only does the song display all of Garland's talents for vocalizing emotions and building a narrative through lyrics and phrasing, it also sets a tone for the entire film. The man "will get away," just as Judy sings. Things will not work out the way they should, "it's all a crazy game." This song was also composed by Harold Arlen, but with lyrics by Ira Gershwin. The tone, like "Over the Rainbow," is mournful, even dirge-like. The lyrics seem to be paradoxically about both facing a harsh reality ("The writing's on the wall, The dreams that you dream have all gone astray") along with hoping against hope that things will turn out differently ("The hope you burn up, Tomorrow he might turn up"). As Dyer writes, "Garland works in an emotional register of great intensity which seems to bespeak equally suffering and survival, vulnerability and strength, theatricality and authenticity, passion and irony ... this passion-with-irony is another inflection of the gay inflection, a doubleness" (155). This doubleness, apparent in my reading of "Over the Rainbow," here operates on several levels. While the song is performed as a torch song about hopeless and disappointed love, the title of the song reveals its hopefulness. Although physically the man has gotten away, he is in fact right there, within the singer's psyche, within the way the song moves and sounds. Her performance suggests that a relationship gone wrong still leaves its mark, still remains part of an experience that can't be eradicated. The milieu of songs describing a love affair with a man going wrong may resonate for gay men precisely because of the historically homophobic conditions in which gay men try to forge relationships with each other. So one of the ironies (and pain) of the man that got away, is that in fact, he remains. Another doubleness is that Garland was singing about a man, and as Dyer puts it, "Gay men gravitated to women singers because they sang of men" (155). There is then a doubleness of identification with Garland, and the Garland impersonator, who is in fact a man. It is because of the doubleness of both Garland's performances and how they comment upon her own biography that she makes such a fitting subject of drag impersonation. Dyer writes, "Garland is imitable, her appearance and gestures copiable in drag acts . . . her later histrionic style can be welcomed as wonderfully over-the-top . . . She is not a star turned into camp, but a star who expresses camp attitudes" (178). As a gay man quoted in Dyer's chapter puts it, "Every time she sang, she poured out her troubles. Life had beaten her up and it showed. This is what attracted homosexuals to her. She created hysteria for them" (150). I would argue that it is in a drag performance of Judy Garland that all the doubleness can display itself. A drag queen dressed up like Judy Garland not only historicizes the very practice of drag with gay male identity, but also historicizes various periods of gay history, before and after Stonewall. The drag performer-as-Judy singing "The Man that Got Away" can sing "for" gay men who know the truth about relationships gone wrong, which can find no expression. The drag performer-as-Judy singing "Over the Rainbow" comments on various levels about childhood innocence, and also about adult longings, about a utopia without alienation and hatred. For those who doubt the efficacy of such representations of hope in despair, the very weekend Judy Garland died at the age of 47 in June 1969, was the beginning of the Stonewall Riots.

Dreams of Glamor, Dreams of Rage

Paris is Burning, a documentary directed by Jennie Livingston, was the art house hit of 1990 and became an important example of what was becoming defined as the New Queer Cinema. Despite these films' progressive intentions, *Paris is Burning* is one of the few New Queer Cinema films that directly and complexly dealt with race at all in an unavoidably queer context. Even some of the more radical versions of the New Queer Cinema by Todd Haynes (*Poison*) or Gregg Araki (*The Living End*) were much more timid, if not mute, on the representational difficulties of race and sexuality.

Paris is Burning can be thought of as functioning as a type of critique on the increasing euphoria around queer representation at the time—it offered a more sobering and artistically complicated vision of queer urban life. I discuss *Paris is Burning* as a way to explore how it dealt with issues of race *and* queerness at the same time. While at times bleak, the film's portrait of race has utopian aspirations that mirror for me the utopian gestures of drag and queer practice itself.

Gender and Race Troubles

Released almost simultaneously as Madonna's hit single, "Vogue," *Paris is Burning* celebrates Black and Latino drag queens and transsexuals who held "voguing" balls and competitions in Harlem in the late 1980s and early 1990s. "Voguing" is a dance form that consists of a series of poses struck by the performer in campy imitation of a high fashion catwalk. The dance fad achieved its widest circulation through Madonna's accompanying video, but it was Livingston's film which offered a more meaningful context for the art form and the complexities of race, class, and gender.

The film emerged in the milieu of the identity politics and culture wars of the late 1980s and early 1990s, where questions of identity and race were hotly debated both in the academy and other cultural and artistic institutions. One of the most influential books on this subject was Judith Butler's 1991 book, *Gender Trouble: Feminism and the Subversion of Identity*. On the first page of her book Butler argues, "For the most part, feminist theory has assumed that here is some existing identity, understood through the category of women, who not only initiates feminist interests and goals within discourse, but constitutes the subject for who political representation is concerned" (1). Butler goes on to state that "gender is not always constituted coherently or consistently in different historical contexts, and because gender intersects with racial, class, ethnic, sexual, and regional modalities of discursively constituted identities." As is evident from the philosophical language, Butler's book is almost forbiddingly dense, but I would like to focus on two specific ideas which are most productive in working through race and gender, and to my point, of thinking through the utopian possibilities posed in *Paris is Burning*.

These two points are: (1) Queer practices may only superficially resemble heterosexual ones, or even feminist ones. In fact, queer drag may have very little to do with gender subversion as it is understood in strictly heterosexual terms. (2) Drag can be liberatory in its derailing of gender assumptions but it often partakes in oppressive narratives of gender, race, and class. These two critical, even opposing, points provide *Paris is Burning* with its spectatorial charge that still gives it an oppositional stance more than ten years later. In 1990 and 1991, questions of race, gender, and queerness aligned in a particularly urgent way in many cultural texts, and *Paris is Burning* provided visible and entertaining representations of these theoretical and activist struggles.

In fact, by decentering essentialist readings of gender identities, by suggesting that "we dispense with the priority of 'man' and 'woman' as abiding substances," Butler opens up different contexts in which to consider *Paris is Burning*. If, for example, we detach, however imaginatively, the concept of masculinity from men, we draw upon the ability of queer people to fashion and refashion identities and practices that may only superficially resemble heterosexual constructs. In this case, a gay marriage may not simply be an imitation of a heterosexual legal and religious union. It may draw upon some (or most) of the elements of convention but also may reinvent ways to construct a commitment or imagine heretofore unimagined forms a relationship could take. This way of re-working heterosexual meanings allows us to reconsider, for example, a gay man's claim that he only wants to find a husband, cook for him, and live in a house with a white picket fence. The very conventionality of this wish, and its reliance upon bourgeois standards of contentment, takes on an entirely different inflection in *Paris is Burning*, which baffled (and baffles still) many critics with its representations of material dreams of wealth and stardom. Considering that Livingston struggled for at least six years to assemble footage and funding, simply the release of the film itself was a triumph of determination and visibility, which resembles the struggles depicted in the film to achieve "stardom."

The participants in the film are shown in a drag environment, dressing up, sewing clothes, applying make-up, and gossiping about each other. The film, of course, has many displays of voguing, but the larger context is that of the competitive atmosphere of the drag ball itself. The cultural sensationalism of drag attracts many viewers to the film, but it is the racial and class dynamics of the performers that give the film its gravity and provide the greatest attraction for cultural critics in the academy.

In the film, not one person is marked visibly as white. The only white images are quick edit clips of rich New Yorkers walking on Park Avenue, glossy magazine photographs, and the cast of TV's *Dynasty*. The juxtaposition between how the queens in the film "really" live and the fantasies they live inside gave many reviewers a charge, and not always a positive one. For example, a prominent character in the film is Octavia, a young black transsexual, who describes her life and dreams quite frankly: "I'd always see the way rich people live, and I'd feel it more, you know, it would slap me in the face, I'd say, 'I have to have that,' because I never felt comfortable being poor, I just don't, or even middle-class doesn't suit me. Seeing the riches, seeing the way people on *Dynasty* lived, these huge houses and I would think, these people have 42 rooms in their house, Oh my God, what kind of house is that, and we've got three. So why is it that they can have that and I didn't? I always felt cheated. I always felt cheated out of things like that." Another seeker of fame and fortune, Venus Xtravaganza, a young Latina transsexual, is also clear about her dreams: "I want to be a spoiled rich white girl . . . I don't want to have to struggle for finances . . . I want a car. I want to be with the man I love. I want a nice home away from New York . . . I want my sex change." A veteran of the ball scene, Dorian Carey remarks that "some of these kids don't even eat—they come to the ball starving . . . but whatever you want to be, you be." Carey's remark is notable because it connects a material reality of physical suffering with the fantasy of dreaming-up another identity, one that is not starving. This contradiction of consciousness that the participants in the film express received different critical responses ranging from cheering to condemnation.

In a generally positive review for *The New York Times*, Vincent Canby described a "terrible sadness in the testimony" and concluded, "the queens knock themselves out to imitate the members of a society that will not have them." But bell hooks, in *Z* magazine, was especially piqued by the film: "Within the world of the black gay drag ball culture she depicts, the idea of womanness and femininity is totally personified by whiteness . . . This combination of class and race longing that privileges the 'femininity' of the ruling-class white woman, adored and kept, shrouded in luxury, does not imply a critique of patriarchy" (148). In fact, hooks sees the entire cultural structure of the drag balls as "contaminated" by a colonizing whiteness: "The whiteness celebrated in *Paris is Burning* is not just any old brand of whiteness but rather that brutal imperial ruling-class patriarchal whiteness that presents itself—its way of life—as the only meaningful life there is" (149). hooks reads the participant's claims straightforwardly and seeks to expose the buried reactionary contexts of their dreams. With a different perspective, academic critic, John Champagne wrote in his book, *The Ethics of Marginality: A New Approach to Gay Studies*,

> The film's relationship to this common-sense desire for wealth and fame is necessarily ambiguous and complicated. Although the interviewed subjects often speak of their desires for wealth and glamour, the film portrays, in what this context seems a highly critical light, white consumer culture, its distance from their "real" lives; and the lures that it continues to hold out and to deny to them . . . The juxtaposition of the men's expressed desires with the realities of their economic interest suggests a critique of the ideology in which balls are necessarily positioned. (108)

Since hooks sees the film as *cinema verite*, she views the fantasies as retrograde and as evidence of a flawed consciousness; Champagne, on the other hand, sees the film as primarily symbolic of the social order, and therefore, too elusive to provide evidence of reactionary politics. These positions can be seen as two sides of the same coin: they both look through the film, wanting to see critical value in what are basically quite tawdry and commercial dreams contained in a small and underbudgeted documentary.

Judith Butler, in her sequel to *Gender Trouble, Bodies That Matter: On the Discursive Limits of "Sex,"* devotes an entire chapter to *Paris is Burning*. Drawing upon Foucualt's formulation of the productivity of power, Butler looks at the film for "what it suggests about the simultaneous production and subjugation of subjects in a culture which appears to arrange always and in every way for the annihilating norms, those killing ideals of gender and race, are mimed, reworded, resignified" (124). Butler recognizes that the oppression(s) caused by racial and economic exploitation can produce a counter-narrative; the creativity displayed in the drag pageants is made possible by the very exploitation that makes them necessary. Butler focuses on how at the end of the film, the viewer discovers that Venus Xtravaganza was brutally murdered by one of her tricks and not found for three days and poses this important question: "Venus, and *Paris is Burning* more generally, calls into question whether parodying the dominant norms is enough to displace them; indeed whether the denaturalization of gender cannot be the very vehicle for a reconsolidating of hegemonic norms." Butler is suggesting that the very displacement of gender norms can lead to a strengthening of those norms. Here, Venus' murder is a means for thinking through the limitation of drag as a "political" response: "I want to emphasize that here is no necessary relation between drag and subversion . . . At best it seems, drag is a site of certain ambivalence, one which reflects the more general situation of being implicated in the regimes of power by which one is constituted and, hence, of being implicated in the very regimes of power one opposes" (125). Butler does not take an either/or position regarding this ambivalence about drag:

> It seems to me that there is both a sense of defeat and a sense of insurrection to be had from the drag pageantry in *Paris is Burning*, that the drag we see . . . is one which both appropriates and subverts racist, misogynist, and homophobic norms of oppression. How are we to account for this ambivalence? This is not first an appropriation and then a subversion. Sometimes it is both at once; sometimes it is caught in an irresolvable tension, and sometimes a fatally unsubversive appropriation takes place. (128)

hooks, too, noted this ambivalence in the film, claiming that it was seen as "inherently oppositional because of its subject matter and the identity of the filmmaker." hooks' point is well taken, but she describes ambivalence as a negative criticism: "Yet the film's politics of race, gender, and class are played out in ways both progressive and reactionary" (149). (It is worth wondering what film, or any cultural production, does not contain elements that could be considered both "progressive and reactionary.") Champagne, meanwhile, criticizes hooks for not privileging this ambiguity in the film: "hooks' reading of drag in *Paris is Burning* fails to recognize how this very idealized, fetishized sexist version of femininity is what Livingston's film both celebrates and critiques, insisting on the pleasures it provides, while also implicating it in such things as the death of Venus." Champagne then offers his own critique of drag: "I would suggest here that drag is not a politically oppositional practice, but one that might by mobilized in the service of, and connected up to, struggles both politically opposition and reactionary" (120).

Racial Dreams/Racial Nightmares

In all these critical accounts what seems to be at stake is the question of whether or not drag, with its context of theatricality, performance, and illusion, is or can be an oppositional practice. For these critics, whether or not drag can offer any version of "politics" will determine its inherent critical importance. But what this film does not ignore is the racial context of these pageants—I think that the issues raised concerning this film are tightly linked with race and racial identity. In fact, *Paris is Burning* can be read as a complete immersion in a nonwhite discourse.

By extension, what else seems to be at stake is the question of the value of sheer fantasy and of wish fulfillment on the part of queers of color. When Venus says she wants to be a "rich spoiled white girl," her wish is compounded not only by her economic and racial subjugation, but also by her gender: she knows she needs a sex change to be a "total woman." This does not fit into the critical context of drag, but to that of transgender politics, which is ignored by all the critics that I have read, who are distracted by the familiar drag theatricality of the film. Venus' wish to be white is harshly criticized by hooks as purely symptomatic of a colonized Fanonian consciousness, and subsequently, this is seen as her retrograde wish to be a white woman. However, in Venus' eyes, this is the same thing. In terms of the film, this is not to say that all those who want to dress up or want to be a woman also want to be white, but that the identity of race becomes as unfixed as a masquerade.

In *Paris is Burning*, it is not just gender which is being denaturalized but also race at the same time. What seems to be irksome for some critics, however, is that the quality of the fantasies in the film seems to be far from revolutionary. It is the content of the dreams and the aspirations which are expressed in the film that seem to provoke the most critical comment.

I wish that many of the commentators and critics of the film had not ignored one of its most visible and winning aspects—the relationship of race with fashion and fashionableness. It seems taken for granted that the participants in the balls are simply practicing a type of parody of high fashion catwalking instead of actually *creating* it. Towards the end of the film, Venus goes to an open call by Eileen Ford for new models looking pretty and a little forlorn, but she clearly holds her own with the gaggle of eager white women. This little moment is important to me, as it shows the clearest mixture of dreams and reality. The highly stylized strut of the fashion runway in fact does not seem so removed from the highly stylized world the kids live in, as they theatrically insult each other, haughtily proclaim their "realness," and generally make mischief, smoking and gossiping. I feel that critics have ignored this texture of the fashion world, along with passing over the possibility that these kids of color would have followed the fashion world. One of the lessons for me of cultural studies is that mass culture spreads information along with its relentless shilling, and it is entirely conceivable that some of the kids would read *Vogue*, be able to identify with various supermodels, have a fairly sophisticated sense of how fame and publicity work, and want to be considered fashionable.

Some commentators discuss the film's declamation of "realness" in philosophical terms, but it is worth noting that the kids' use of "realness" does not involve any type of recognizable "real" behavior. The "realness" they incorporate into daily life is intensely stylized and informs every exaggerated expression they display, not only their catwalking. There is very little distinction between drag "realness" and what constitutes the kids' "real life." The relationship of fashion with the street and fashion to the avant-garde is not an entirely degraded one—I am willing to hold out that the legitimacy the kids seek from the grammar of the fashion world is not entirely one-sided. Fashion has also historically drawn legitimacy and relevancy from the streets and youth culture.

But however mediated, *Paris is Burning* does offer new possibilities for different narratives. It is interesting, then, to consider how depressing the film actually is. AIDS is not explicit in the film, but its ravages are there in the subtext, adding to the material and emotional suffering. When confronted with the drag queens and transsexuals of color in *Paris is Burning*, one is confronted with the collision of race and sexuality—and poverty. The kinds of wishful aspirations that are produced in this context are necessarily formed and reformed and deformed by exploitation. In fact, the gritty sheen of the film's texture contributes to its ambience not just as "reality," but as a resourceful use of materials at hand.

Racial Utopia

I argue that if drag is an instance of gender denaturalization, and a site of affective investment and historical context, in *Paris is Burning*, race becomes a signifier of utopian longings. The wish to be "white," seems in this case, not simply a psychological pathology, but also a sense of not wanting to be what one is—poor, abject. How exactly gender as an aspiration is imprecated cannot be made entirely clear, but I do think that in this film, race contains its own fantasies of displacement and escape. In this context, it is *stardom* which is supposed to fulfill all the longings that poverty and racism create.

For me, the longings for stardom, for comfort from suffering in the film remain unrequited. To want to change what one is, to inhabit another space more comfortable and beautiful, a place that may contain 42 rooms and where a boy is a girl and a girl is a boy is not simply a reactionary wish. In fact, it seems a fairly reasonable one. That in this film these wishes take place in a space of racial marginalization, through the "terrible markers of race and gender," makes them much more poignant, and perhaps more impossible to fulfill. The film's longing for something better and for something different is particularly resonant for me in terms of AIDS. The memory of losses known and unknown, recorded and unrecorded are practically unspeakable for queers of color.

Perhaps sexual identities "feel" different when expressed through desires and race; racial identities may "feel" different when experienced through poverty and sexuality. What *Paris is Burning* makes poetically clear is that wish fulfillment cannot follow any straightforward political trajectory. This is what makes longing and dream making such potent and dangerous cultural tools, perhaps leading to unpredictable new manifestations of utopian possibilities and new considerations of queer identities.

Chapter 4

Kiss: Utopian Romance and Manuel Puig's Spider Woman

Manuel Puig's novel, *Kiss of the Spider Woman*, was published in 1976 and in it circulate questions about Hollywood fantasies, political injustice, and unrequited love all in one of the most austere narrative frames possible: a prison cell. It seems to me that the unrequited intensity of the material is precisely what seems to elude its many critics and the various adaptations it has undergone. For example, in Brazilian director Hector Babenco's film version of the book, released in 1986, the erotic charge of the book is absent. William Hurt plays Molina, the gay movie fan, and Raul Julia plays Valentin, the straight revolutionary. William Hurt plays his *idea* of a gay man, which means talking huskily, walking with one hand on his hip, and wearing a towel like a turban on his head. It is not so much his stereotypical mannerisms that jar me as much as the extremely low energy level at which Hurt plays Molina. Hurt is not a very expressive actor, and his deadpan, levelheaded, WASPishness is all wrong for a gay character who is practically drunk on movies and fantasies of romantic love. The acclaim that Hurt received for the role (he won a Best Actor award at both Cannes and the Academy Awards) seemed to stem from his *daring* to play a gay man at all. This self-serving aspect of his performance is evidenced by the character's unrelenting seriousness. Nowhere is there any indication that Molina gets any pleasure from even thinking about movies, not to mention elaborating upon them. What is also missing is an understanding of the relationship between expressive camp and the movies, which has to do with the "queer" perspective of Puig's novel.

In representing the two men's relationship, the movie over-emphasizes the differences between them, and how this causes a serious conflict, until they finally reach a moment of redemption. In the novel their relationship is more ambiguous. They display warmth towards each other, and take an active interest in each other's personal lives. There is a reason that Molina falls in love with Valentin—the kindness they show each other has a resonance that is missing in the film. What the film seems unable to represent in any meaningful way is not only the importance of movies as escape, but the important role movies have played in gay male identity, especially concerning camp, and its reconfiguration of gender, desire, and politics. What *Kiss of the Spider Woman* calls out for is a campy reading, one that takes Puig's material on its own terms. It needs a reading that resists not only the moralistic lesson that although we all need fantasy in our lives, there is no substitute for hard reality, but also one that knows the importance of sentimentality and camp to Puig's project.

In an interview, Puig admitted his reaction to the film of his book was "negative." When pressed why, he replied:

> Because the average spectator who had not read the novel would think the movie was progressive and liberating. But compared with the book, the movie is reactionary. In the book, the character is full of joy and life, and that's missing in the movie. William Hurt created a fascinating character, but not the one in my novel. Hurt created a neurotic and tortured character who has nothing to do with Molina, who was a very joyful person, among other things, and who did not feel the Calvinistic guilt that was attributed to him in the picture. In spite of all this, given the fact homosexuality has always been ridiculed and reduced to putrid characterizations movies, the film can be considered both progressive and liberating. (Gautier 225)

Given Puig's obvious affection for Molina, I would like to consider Molina as a character on his own terms—and within the context of camp that he participates in. I would also like to think through Molina's devotion to movies and how this informs his notions of self and of love.

Manuel Puig

In 1990, when Manuel Puig died at the age of 57 in Cuernavaca, Mexico, *The New York Times* attributed the cause of death to cardiac arrest following a fairly routine gall bladder operation. Speculation immediately arose about the true cause of death. It had been widely and immediately suspected that Puig had died of AIDS complications and that he and a compliant media acted to cover that up. Writing in *Christopher Street* magazine, gay Colombian writer, Jaime Manrique, describes Puig as being openly gay and he speculates that Puig and his immediate family may have acted to cover up the true nature of his death. Manrique writes, "After all, if homosexuality is the greatest taboo in Hispanic culture, AIDS is the unspeakable." Ilan Stavans writes how Puig had moved with his mother to Cuernavaca, "spending the last months of his life, busy building his first and last home in this world, a fortress closed to strangers, filled with Hollywood memorabilia. Puig's death is emblematic of the fate of the Hispanic gay" (158). Stavans' assertion echoes the comments expressed about Arturo Islas' death from AIDS. Is this the Hispanic gay's "fate"? Considering the gay content and thematic in *Kiss of the Spider Woman* alone, not to mention his other novels and stories with gay themes, it would seem almost bizarre to think that Puig was closeted. That the secrecy here seems to be about AIDS, and a retreat from its stigmatizing effects, contributes to a "doubling" of the closet. There is a mourning of the death and a mourning that the death cannot be properly mourned. But within the context of Puig's work, it would also imply another doubling: the death of Molina in the novel is both the obligatory gay martyr of much gay fiction and also a release for Molina into the roles he has always dreamed about.

It is not just Puig's death that seems unable to account for his homosexuality. As I mentioned before, it is the "gayness" of his most famous novel that seems to elude critics. There is a general critical consensus that the major project of his work is to consider the effects and uses of mass culture on "ordinary people." Critic Jonathan Tuttle speaks for most critics: "The name of Manuel Puig has for almost 25 years brought with it associations with popular or mass culture... His enduring innovation, we can safely say now, resides in his incorporating the cultural by-products of certain mid-century technological advancements that, for better or worse, have served to link less developed regions with the metropolitan centers... The diverse effects of these largely commercially inspired, cliché-ridden, and sentimentally oriented mass-entertainment products on often impressionable psyches constitute a hallmark of Puig's creativity" (1). In their book *Memory and Modernity: Popular Culture in Latin America*, Rowe and Schelling describe the use of popular forms such as serials in Puig's work: "Puig's characters are addicted to the stereotyping of radio serials and films, but actively collude in being manipulated, and know very well how to negotiate the gaps between the ideal and the actual: the responsibility is not solely that of the media. Puig's novels introduce desire into the equation" (107). Critics such as these do not see Puig's use of mass culture as negative but instead stress the agency that Puig makes available to his characters to manipulate these forms in turn. What they do not do is give a queer inflection to this use of mass culture. In other words, they do not give an interpretative space to the uses of camp for making sense of popular culture.

As in our discussion of Arturo Islas, it is imperative to emphasize the importance of camp and sentimentality to gay expressive culture. For if Puig's novels are informed by a campy use of mass media forms, his childhood contains elements of camp "knowingness." He was born in 1932 in General Villegas, Argentina, which Puig described as "really stifling, and we felt the need to escape from that environment. Not only was there machismo all over the place, but there was also a total absence of landscape, just dry pampas all over the place." His escape came from the movies, and his "mother would take him every afternoon at six to the only movie theater in town to see mostly American films and would make them live a world of fantasy." In fact, when he was asked as a child what he wanted to be when he grew up, he gave the campiest of answers: "a movie." It could be argued that to "be a movie" is to inhabit the essence of camp: it is to participate intensely in a world of artificiality. The irony about this contradiction makes it camp. Also when asked as a child to list his favorite stars, they usually consisted of Ingrid Bergman, Greta Garbo, Rita Hayworth, and Ginger Rogers (Gautier 119).

Puig's idolization of glamorous female Hollywood stars implies a type of drag identification, or at least a camp identification with beauty and intensity. His first novel *Betrayed by Rita Hayworth* takes place in the Argentinean pampas, and contains a character named Toto, who, as a prototype of Molina, finds refuge from his harsh surroundings in *cosas lindas* ("pretty things"). It may seem that the overbearing mother has been replaced, or at least nudged aside, by an early devotion to the movies as a facile explanation for male homosexuality. In fact, heterosexually normative readings will inflect a critic's (mis)understanding not only of Puig's project, but his characters, such as Molina. Critic Pamela Bacarisse points out that Toto and Molina are "both victims of spatial limitations, of a mother fixation, and of the imbalance caused by the absence of a father figure. Then, although there are many points of divergence between them, we should not forget that almost everything in Toto's childhood points towards homosexuality in his adult life, and effeminate homosexuality at that" (87).

All this reads as clinical psychology disguised as literary criticism, but in my reading, Puig actually sees little about Toto or Molina that is pathological or condemnatory. In Bacarisse's estimation, it is the pathology of these characters' effeminacy that has to be accounted for, but I would like to think about how Molina's effeminacy becomes his most powerful and durable weapon. Molina's characteristics which could be described as effeminate include: intense devotion to mother; close attentiveness to details of style and decor; habit of reproducing mannerisms in a slightly exaggerated way; sensitivity, especially toward criticism or neglect; generosity, especially with those he is trying to please; passiveness toward men, both sexual and emotional; attraction to the melodramatic and the emotionally sensational; fear of aggression and violence, especially explosive outbursts; self-deprecation about conventionally male values such as bravery, cleverness, and steadfastness; fondness of luxuries and comforts; reluctance to distinguish between fantasy and reality, or between triviality and importance; an inability to take seriously what is most publicly important, as opposed to emotionally private.

In *Kiss of the Spider Woman* Puig wanted to think about these effeminate characteristics, especially in light of debates about male power, feminism, and male homosexuality. As he discussed in an interview:

> Around 1972, discussions on feminism became more frequent in Argentina. I was totally in agreement with this process. I was concerned, however, that people were only talking about the inconveniences of being oppressed women, and never of the advantages, since there had to be some for such an unnatural situation to last for centuries. I believe that in a war, one should never underestimate the enemy's weapons; therefore, I wanted to know what those weapons were. So I had to find out what could make them both happy and oppressed. I wanted to find such a woman, to turn her into the heroine of my next novel. (224)

Puig describes his subsequent search, which ends with his inability to find "one single woman who was completely satisfied with her role as an oppressed being." At first thinking that therefore he could not write his novel, he relates that although he:

> ... didn't find a female voice, I did discover an effeminate one, a certain type of homosexual with a feminine fixation who would still defend the traditional state of things. Since it was impossible for him to get married, this homosexual could still find solace in the role of defenseless being vis-à-vis a "strong" man who would protect him. I remembered terrible things in that period of the forties when women expressed themselves in such terms as "I cannot love a man if I do not fear him a little when he embraces me." In other words, eroticism was absolutely associated with domination, and people thought this was a completely natural state of affairs. (225)

I do not think Puig means to disguise Molina, that Molina is in fact "really" a woman. I think instead that he deliberately constructs a gay character that can call into question all assumptions about gender and sexuality. Perhaps Molina is a woman, but also a gay man. It is Molina's participation in a gay camp discourse that distinguishes or identifies him as "gay." Indeed, Puig's project is much too complex to reduce to a gender misidentification. But in fact, critics such as Bacarisse place Molina in a simplified context with other female Puig characters:

> Though there is more to him than his sexuality, this is undeniably what is most immediately distinctive about him, and at the same time, it causes him to be fatuous, pathetic, and touching... In other words, he is another of Puig's female characters... he embodies sexual exploitation. He is another ill-used woman, glad to suffer—or, at the very least, prepared to suffer at the hands of a "superior" man. (96. All quotes from the novel are taken from the Thomas Colchie translation from the Original Spanish, 1991)

Bacarisse is too quick to place Molina into a heterosexual female context. Here, in the space of the novel, and in the context of gay camp, the category of "woman" itself is being challenged and de-naturalized. Molina himself in the novel addresses how people are:

> Always coming to me with the same business, always! How they spoiled me too much as a kid, and that's why I'm the way I am, how I was tied to my mother's apron strings and now I'm this way, and how a person can always straighten out though, and what I really need is a woman, because a woman's the best there is... and my answer is this... great! I agree! And since a woman's the best there is... I want to be one. (19. All quotes from the novel are taken from the Thomas Colchie translation from the original Spanish, 1991)

Molina expresses how he knows effeminacy is seen as a pathology for which there must be a cause and a cure. Various psychoanalytic theories of maternal overdependence and the heterosexual imperative are confronted by Molina with what seems like acquiescence. But Molina's response—"I want to be one"—is not the expected normative one. He has coyly and comically manipulated the terms that were offered by "them." By homosexualizing the heterosexist terms of his development, Molina manages to retain some agency. Valentin responds characteristically, "I don't see it so clear, at least not the way you worked it out" (19). But by the end, Valentin will become much more of a participant in Molina's gendering project.

I now turn to the novel itself, where I will concentrate on the relationship that Molina and Valentin build with each other and the echoes it finds in the movies Molina tells. I choose this emphasis because while their relationship is quite obviously the focus of the narrative, many critics seem to see right through it. Instead of looking through the relationship, seeing it merely as a transcendence of gender and sexuality and race, I want to examine the particular queer dynamics of what exactly Valentin and Molina construct.

The Cell

When Puig published *Kiss of the Spider Woman*, it was immediately banned in Argentina. As Santiago Colas points out in his *Postmodernity in Latin America: The Argentine Paradigm*, that very year, a "military coup headed by General Videla ousted the discredited regime of Isabel Peron. The following seven years were known as the Process of National Reorganization, or simple as the 'Proceso.' The military government terrorized, tortured, disappeared, and killed tens of thousands of Argentines, and million fled the country in exile—all the in the name of a doctrine of national purification" (76). Colas, while pointing out this was the first of Puig's explicitly "political" novels, also sees it as "prophetically" confronting the reality of the *guerra suicia* ("dirty war"). Puig himself addressed how the political regime in his country affected the distribution of his novel: "*Kiss of the Spider Woman* was not read in Argentina almost until the movie came out, because the junta and the post-junta managed to discredit me so that I no longer had a name and no one knew me or was interested in my work . . ." The novel, though, never directly addresses any specific political issue. The sentiment of it, however, and its fierce lack of faith in masculinist authority must have been enough to render it suspect to the State if they were careful enough readers. The irony, too, is that the novel's main inhabitant is Molina, who expressly, if not vehemently, avoids any type of political engagement. In fact, once he finally decides to act in an overtly political way, he is destroyed before he can even commit an effective action.

The novel takes place almost entirely in a prison cell, shared by Molina, imprisoned for molesting a minor, and Valentin, a straight Marxist revolutionary, imprisoned and tortured for crimes against the oppressive state. In the cell itself, Molina passes the time, or rather, escapes from the cell by narrating to Valentin, and to himself, the plots and details of movies he remembers seeing. Valentin spends his days studying Marxist economic theory, completely dedicated to political change. When Valentin interrupts one of Molina's narrations with a critique of a character's economic exploitation, Molina replies, "Look, I'm tired, and it makes me angry the way you brought this all up, because until you brought it up I was feeling fabulous, I'd forgotten all about this filthy cell, and all the rest, just telling you about the film . . . Why break the illusion for me, and for yourself too? What kind of trick is that to pull?" (17). Molina then can use the narrative of the film to feel "fabulous," to escape from the "filthy cell." In this formulation, for Molina there is an "outside" of the cell which contains freedom. Molina can literally visualize this freedom through his films, through illusion, and through narrative itself. He simply cannot understand why someone would not want to participate in this attempt to leave misery.

When Molina tries to distract Valentin from his studies, telling him, "You're crazy, live for the moment! Enjoy life a little!" Valentin replies:

> There's no way I can live for the moment because my life is dedicated to political struggle, or, you know, political action, let's call it . . . I can put up with anything in here, which is quite a lot . . . because there's a purpose behind it. Social revolution, that's what's important, and gratifying the senses is only secondary . . . the great pleasure's something else, it's knowing I've put myself in the service of what's truly noble . . . My ideals . . . Marxism, if you want me to spell it out in only one word. And I can get that pleasure anywhere, right here in this cell, and even in torture. And that's my real strength. (28–29)

Valentin can find his "strength" in his "ideals," and this is what he uses to escape from the reality of the cell, and even of torture. He doesn't see the sensual gratification that Molina prizes as an adequate enough escape, but does negotiate the "reality" of the cell away into something bigger, and more liberatory, in this case Marxism. There are then two utopian narratives being constructed, and defended, here in the cell

The first is the idea of entertainment as utopia. The world of the movies, for Molina, is not about politics, or even psychology. This is what makes them utopian. Politics and psychological explanations serve only to repress and to remove complete engagement with the pleasure at hand. Because Molina as a homosexual knows that pleasure can be policed and degraded by authority, he wants to remove himself from any manifestation of judgment. Movies supply a real-life narrative in which to situate himself: in a movie he can cross genders; he can experience the upper heights of emotional ecstasy with his lover; he can be a brave heroine, or a meek woman who is finally recognized for her beauty; he can be glamorous and adored, along with living life the way he likes; most of all, he can suffer in love for a man—and it can be beautiful. His movies can accommodate contradictions and supply a way of making sense of his life in the cell. They can also be a way of drawing his sexy cell mate into his web of narrative desire. Valentin seems aware of the seduction of these narratives, and that is what he distrusts.

The second idea is that of revolution as utopia. Recognizing the ravages of economic exploitation, Valentin is willing to sacrifice all hope of sensual gratification for a more noble cause. The liberatory project of revolutionary Marxism provides a practical blueprint for achieving a socialist paradise. Within the labyrinth of economic theory, Valentin is convinced, lay the secrets to all mysteries and motives of injustice and poverty. There is nothing that cannot be explained by rational thought and careful dialectic practice. His political engagement makes him feel alive, gives him a sense of higher purpose, and helps him to make sense of his life in the cell. It can also be a way of drawing away from his amorous cell mate. For Valentin the seduction of economic theory may seem less extravagant than that of film, but it may also provide its own consoling narrative.

That both cellmates are involved in their own forms of self-deception, self-deception that is necessary for their survival, is clear. What develops in the novel through their relationship is a transforming of what they expect from the "outside." Colas sees the novel exploring the "construction of utopian spaces; the ways people seek to transcend the restrictive conditions—the prisons—in which they live" (76). He argues that in the novel, "the abstract concept of utopia is brought into crisis . . . For it is simultaneously constructed and deconstructed in the text. The text also inscribes a historical crisis of utopia. The utopian project of the sixties, to generate entirely new spaces free from alienation, remains the only mode of liberation as the novel opens. Freedom involves the occupation of a position 'outside,' whereas repression means staying 'inside.' But by the novel's end this binary logic unravels" (77). One of the ways in which utopia is called into question is in the space of the cell itself. The cell is, of course, the site of their imprisonment, their removal from the world "out there." But as Colas notes, "The firm boundaries between an oppressive existence inside and a liberated existence outside are eroded" (77). A perfect example of this erosion occurs after an argument between the two cell mates.

Molina has been trying to spoil and tease Valentin with sweets and tea, and then Valentin refuses his offer of marble cake:

—Thanks, I don't want any.
—You don't want any . . . Oh, I've heard that before . . .
—Don't be telling me what I have to do . . .
—But, hey, can't I just coddle you a little bit? . . .

—Cut it out! . . . Christ almighty!!!
—You gone crazy? . . . What the hell's wrong with you? (193)

At this point Valentin violently knocks over their little stove, and retreats into himself. When he finally apologizes for his outburst, Valentin has this revelation:

> Yes, but in this case, the two of us are locked up here, so there is no struggle, no fight to win . . . Then are we so pressured . . . by the outside world, that we can't act civilized? Is it possible . . . that the enemy, out there, has so much power? . . . Well, that everything that's wrong with the world . . . and everything that I want to change . . . is it possible all that won't allow me to . . . behave . . . even for a single moment, like a decent human being? I don't know if you understand me . . . but here we are, all alone, and when it comes to our relationship, how should I put it? We could make any damn thing out of it we want; our relationship isn't pressured by anyone . . . In a sense we're perfectly free to behave however we choose with respect to one another . . . It's as if we were on some desert island. An island on which we may have to remain alone together for years. Because, well, outside of this cell we may have our oppressors, yes, but not inside. Here no one oppresses the other . . . (202)

In this extraordinary speech, Valentin has reversed the inside/outside dynamic of the prison cell. Now it is the cell that is the utopian space, and it is the "outside" which oppresses. This "island" of the cell, for Valentin, can be a creative space for constructing different types of relationships, relatively free from domination. He does question, though, "Whether the enemy, out there, has so much power?" The cell in this case reminds one of Michel Foucault's, *Discipline and Punish: The Birth of the Prison*. Through his genealogy of the prison, Foucault offered what was to become one of his most incisive theories: that of power in the modern world. He describes the phenomenon of prison and incarceration as historically contingent. Why did the imprisonment of the body take its place as the logical response to crime, as the most ideal form of punishment, Foucault asks, and he begins outlining the larger implications of the prison for society at large. While refusing to see power as that which exists up above and that dominates all below, Foucault did not believe that power relations could be reversed or usurped. He argued that:

> This power is exercised rather than possessed; it is not the "privilege," acquired or preserved, of the dominant class, but the over all effect of its strategic positions—an effect that is manifested and sometimes extended

by the position of those who are dominated. Furthermore, this power is not exercised simply as an obligation or a prohibition on those who "do not have it"; it invests them is transmitted by them and through them; it exerts pressure upon them, just as they themselves, in their struggle against it, resist the grip it has on them. This means that these relations go right down into the depths of society . . . (27)

Power then inhabits all aspects of society, both macro and micro, but this power is not always a negative, oppressive force, pushing down upon its unwilling subjects. Impatiently, Foucault declares, "We must cease once and for all to describe the effects of power in negative terms: it 'excludes,' it 'represses,' it 'censors,' it 'abstracts,' it 'masks,' it 'conceals.' In fact power produces; it produces reality; it produces domains of objects and rituals of truth" (194). Power then not only produces the conditions of oppression, it also produces the conditions to resist it. To think of power permeating every crevice of everyday life, from the civil to the private, is to be aware of the constant dynamism of power itself. Power is just not located in the "relations between the state and its citizens," but instead comes to "define innumerable points of confrontation, focuses of instability, each of which has its own risks of conflict, of struggles, and of at least temporary inversion of the power relations" (27). It is these "points of confrontation" that contain their own sites of struggle and potential: "The overthrow of these 'micropowers' does not, then, obey the law of all or nothing; it is not acquired once and for all by a new control of the apparatuses" (27). A power struggle then is never settled, and power can be taken—but never decisively. This concept of various "networks" of power offers the possibility of resistance at every level of political and social life. Of course, this means also conceiving resistance in varied and unpredictable forms. The question of making social and political changes on more than the microlevel is a matter of linking of these various sites: "On the other hand, none of its localized episodes may be inscribed in history except by the effects that it induces on the entire network on which it is caught up" (27). The series of "webs" then must connect up in order to affect the "web," on which larger changes can be made. It is, of course, an open question on how exactly to link these resistances without resorting to institutional forms, or in Marx's terms, without changing the modes of production. In this sense, Molina's terms of illusion seem to be at best half-hearted, but they are part of a web, perhaps of resistance.

When Valentin describes the cell he shares with Molina as an "island" away from repressive power, he is unable to see how power is indeed inside this utopia. He doesn't know that Molina has been negotiating with the prison guards for his own release if he can give them information about Valentin and his revolutionary group. Valentin also believes that the delicious food that Molina brings back after his meetings with the prison officials is from his mother. But the groceries are in fact provided by the prison itself in order to maintain the sham and inadvertently make Valentin complicit. While Molina is unable ultimately to betray Valentin because of his love for him, he does entangle himself into a web of deceit and desire. The larger web that is woven, however, is that which traps both the cellmates. They have failed to grasp that the most intimate aspects of life—love, lust, desire, happiness—are also manifestations of power. Valentin's Marxism leaves him unable to account for the emotional world that Molina seduces him to inhabit; Molina's films leave him unable to cope with undertaking decisive political action, or to see how infused with power relations are the scenes he narrates from his favorite films. But the final scene of the book confirms the importance of dreaming—the necessity of dreaming—if one is to resist power at all.

Molina's Movies

Considering the points I have made about the importance of Hollywood cinema and fantasy to Puig's project, it is interesting that the specific movies represented in *Kiss of the Spider Woman* are hardly extravagant Hollywood productions. They are instead "small" B-movies, with no major Hollywood stars which are narrated by Molina with detail and feeling. Formally, Puig might be emphasizing the texture of films, their reception in the audience's imagination, and their ability to affect consciousness. Throughout the course of the novel, Molina narrates six films, five of which are described by Puig as illustrations of the "various clichés of femininity." The first film is generally considered the most important by many critics, *Cat People*. The rest are: a Nazi propaganda film; *The Enchanted Cottage*; a film about a privileged revolutionary, narrated only to himself; *I Walked with a Zombie*; a Mexican melodrama about a journalist who destroys himself, a beautiful kept woman who ends up being a streetwalker, and the Spider woman, who appears to Valentin at the end of book.

Two other narrative discourses also impose themselves on the script, (1) that of the textual footnotes, detailing a type of political and social theory and debate of homosexuality, and (2) the meetings between Molina and the prison officials. While I do not have the space in which to fully explore these dynamics, they will, as in the novel, intrude upon the narratives at hand. I will instead describe two of the films, *Cat People* and the Nazi propaganda film and try to suggest what they might say about the larger web of the book. By describing the contents of these films, they will cumulatively act as an important component to the "feeling" of the novel. It will also lead to a discussion of the relationship between Molina and Valentin, within the context of the cell and the movies narrated in it.

The novel opens with Molina narrating *Cat People*, an actual 1942 low-budget horror production, directed by Jacques Tourneur, produced by Val Lewton, and starring Simone Simon. Molina begins his narration with, "Something a little strange, that's what you notice, that she's not a woman like all the others" (3). Molina becomes very involved in the plot of the film, which concerns young, mysterious Irena, who falls in love with an architect who is drawn to her, despite her strangeness. They meet, when on a blustery cold day, she is sketching a panther in its cage at the zoo. She seems mesmerized by the animal. They eventually marry, but Irena refuses to sleep with him because she is convinced that she carries an ancient Carpathian curse that will turn her into a murderous cat if she merely kisses someone. Her husband is concerned for her and confides in a woman that he works with, who obviously carries feelings for him. Irena, consults a psychiatrist, who in turn, obviously has designs on her. (Molina describes him approvingly as an obvious Lothario.) Irena stops seeing her psychiatrist, her marriage deteriorates, and she begins to suspect that her husband is having an affair with the pretty, but simple, assistant. Driven to a jealous rage, she stalks the assistant, in the guise of a large menacing panther, but misses in her attempt to maul her. Finally a meeting is arranged, after Irena has been missing for some time, and caught alone with the psychiatrist, she turns into a panther and kills him when he kisses her. She flees to the zoo, and lets the panther she drew at the start of the film free which then kills her and escapes before finally being shot. The film ends with the husband and the assistant walking off together into some type of contented "normality," with the beasts now safely out of the way.

Since this is the first film and the first section of the novel, it operates narratively to establish the relationship between Molina and Valentin. Valentin seems very interested and often interjects comments on the obvious psychoanalytic aspects of the film, which Molina instantly and instinctually rejects. When Molina relates how Irena refuses to sleep with her husband, saying that "to become a real wife to him, she asks him to give her a little time, until all those fears have a chance to subside . . ." Valentin interrupts with, "You get what's going on, don't you?... I think she's frigid, she's afraid of men, either that or she has some idea about sex that's really violent, and so she invents things" (16). When Molina chides him for interrupting with his comments, Valentin replies, "I like the picture, but you have the fun of telling it and I just want to chime in once in a while too, see what I mean... I'd like us to discuss the thing a little, as you go on with it, so I get the chance now and then to rap about something... it could be just a simple discussion" (16–17). Valentin here clearly identifies the pleasure that Molina receives from telling the story and wants to participate in his own pleasure, that of taking the story apart to examine and expose its dynamics.

Valentin is interested in the psychological and economic motives of the characters in Molina's films, and in this one, he offers a perfectly Oedipal one. When he asks Molina how he pictures the man's mother (who is not in the film, except when Molina says that he pictures the apartment that the hero lives in as furnished with her furniture and decor), Molina replies, "A lovely lady, who gave her husband every happiness and her children too, always managing everything perfectly... I see her as impeccably attired, a dress with a high collar... She has that marvelous thing of certain respectable ladies, which is that touch of coquettishness, beneath all the properness." Valentin replies with his own reading:

> Yes, always impeccable. Perfect. She has her servants, she exploits people who can't do anything else but serve her, for a few pennies. And clearly she felt very happy with her husband, who in turn exploited her, forced her to do whatever he wanted, keeping her cooped up in a house like a slave, waiting for him—... waiting for him every night, until he got back from his law firm or his doctor's office. And she was in perfect agreement with the whole system, and she didn't rebel, and she fed her own son the same crap and now the son runs smack into the panther woman. Good luck with that one. (16–17)

It is here that Molina rebels against Valentin's crude analysis (which as some pop psychologist might suggest reveals his own "issues"), since he sees it as interfering with his "feeling fabulous" and his having "forgotten all about this filthy cell."

Valentin's interruptions into Molina's filmic narration operate in at least two important ways. First, they serve to illustrate Valentin's character as the rational voice; the voice that can articulate the class-consciousness of Molina's stories to which he is indifferent, if not ignorant. Valentin sees the film as "making sense... it's just like an allegory, and really clear too, of the woman's fear of giving in to a man, because by completely giving in to sex she reverts a little to an animal" (31). In this sense, they act to further schematize the two characters. Molina equals frivolous, overly romantic, lost in fantasy, and generally too caught up in the story and its emotions to see how he is being manipulated or to "read" narrative as metaphor or allegory. Valentin equals serious, overly analytic, lost in the process of critique, able to "decode" surface meaning into its larger implications, and generally too caught up in the politics of the story to see how it might "mean" something to Molina. But as the novel progresses, Valentin's interruptions will actually become less crudely and patronizingly articulated, and he begins to read the movies in a different, more nuanced way.

Second, Valentin's interruptions prompt discussions about identification with the characters in the movies. The two will begin relating who it is they desire in the film, and who it is they desire to be. After his exasperation with Valentin's outburst about the hero's Oedipal complex, Molina complains, "Why couldn't I have the luck to get the panther woman's boyfriend to keep me company, instead of you?" (17). This leads directly to a conversation about each of their sexualities, and their character identifications:

—Oh, now that's another story, and I'm not interested.
—Afraid to talk about such things?
—No, not afraid. Just not my bag. I already know all about yours, even if you didn't tell me a thing.
—Well, I told you what I'm in for, corruption of minors, and that tells it all, so don't start playing the psychological now.
—Come on, admit it, you like him because he smokes a pipe.
—No, because he's the gentle type, and understanding.
—His mother castrated him, plain and simple.
—I like him and that's enough for me. And you, you like the assistant, some urban guerrilla that one!
—I like her, sure, more than the panther woman. (17)

I do not think that here Valentin demonstrates overt or immediate hostility towards Molina's homosexuality. In fact he engages him in expressing his desire for the male character, and Molina, in turn, teases him about *his* attractions. This kind of bantering continues throughout the novel, and makes their eventual sexual bonding less "sensationalistic" than some critics insist. In fact, when Molina continues the story, Valentin advises him that "the pipe-smoker's no good for you" (20). When Molina describes Irena's psychiatrist as "incredibly good looking, a fantastic flirt," Valentin interrupts with: "What's your definition of incredibly good-looking? I'd like to hear" (20). This kind of active participation on Valentin's part emphasizes the mutuality behind their relationship. It is not just the describing of the movie that brings them together, but discussions about the desires provoked by the films. These discussions are extra-textual and symbolize the meaning and sense that spectators make about narratives—and how desire can be generated in these productions of meanings.

What else gets provoked by *Cat People* is the issue of gender cross-identification. After asking permission to interrupt, Valentin asks Molina, "Only one question, which intrigues me a little . . . You won't get annoyed? . . . It'd be interesting to know. And afterwards you ask me if you want . . . Who do you identify with? Irena or the other one?" Molina replies promptly and unequivocally, "With Irena, what do you think? She's the heroine, dummy. Always with the heroine." Valentin then admits that he identifies with the psychiatrist in the story, but tells Molina, "no making jokes now, I respected your choice, with no remarks" (25). Even from their little game of identifications, which is set up by Valentin, with his insistence of "respect" for the identifications made by each of them, it is clear how they fantasize about each other. Molina always identifies with the female lead, the heroine, who is the center of adoration and narrative attention. This is a key aspect of camp films, to idolize the strong woman who is shaken by her passions. Valentin sees himself not only as the rational psychiatrist, who is convinced he can see through and cure various maladies caused by weak character, but also as the handsome rake that Molina describes. They have each cast themselves as the leads in a Hollywood movie. Valentin identifies so strongly with the doctor that at one point in Molina's narration, when he becomes unsure of the outcome of the plot, Valentin bursts in, "Don't tell me that at the end the panther woman winds up with me" (32). The seduction then that Molina performs on Valentin vis-à-vis the movies is in fact quite mutual. What else they seem to share is an ability to transfer, or at least project, some part of their identity. In fact, they each have a strong attachment to particular women in their lives and feel frustrated, imprisoned in the cell away from them.

When Molina is describing the architect's assistant running from danger (from Irena), Valentin suddenly withdraws his attention from the story, because he becomes worried about his girlfriend: "When you started telling how the girl was being followed by the panther woman, I pictured that it was my girl who was in danger. And I feel so helpless here, about warning her to be careful, about not taking too many risks."

Molina shares Valentin's apprehension, revealing that, "Me too, you know, I have that sensation, from being in here, of not being able to do anything; but in my case it's not a woman—not a girl I mean, it's my mother . . . she's so sick. She's got high blood pressure and her heart's weak" (35). Valentin is reluctant at first about sharing details about his girl, since she is a revolutionary too. He tells Molina, by way of explanation: "It's just that I don't want to saddle you with any information you're better off not having. It's a burden, and you've already got enough of your own" (35). It will be revealed as the novel progresses that their attachments compromise each of them in particular and crucial ways. Molina is manipulated by the prison officials to get information from Valentin in order for him to get an early release so he can attend to his ailing mother. His increasing attachment to Valentin, however, makes it more difficult, if not impossible, to betray him, even for his own mother. Valentin reveals that there is another woman, Marta, who is beautiful and bourgeois, and that it is she who he truly loves. He despises himself for going against all his principles, for giving into his desire for "superficial," romantic love. Each of these women also emphasize the characters' sexual identities: Molina's devotion to his mother is a stereotype of male homosexuality, and Valentin's estranged lover romanticizes heterosexuality as "true love."

But their attachment to women becomes further compromised by Molina's cross-gender identifications. When Valentin criticizes Molina for being oversensitive, Molina replies that he can't help it, he's "very sentimental." They then have this exchange:

—[Valentin speaking] I'll say. It sounds just like a . . .
—What are you stopping for?
—Nothing.
—Say it, I know what you were going to say.
—Don't be silly.
—Say it, like a woman, that's what you were going to say.
—Yes.
—And what's so bad about being soft like a woman? Why is it men or whoever, some poor bastard, some queen can't be sensitive, too, if he's got a mind to? (29)

Molina is not afraid to identify as a "woman," because he in fact believes that it is only by doing so that he can be "sensitive." He wants to detach himself from male power, and to retreat into what he sees as a safety zone—being a woman. The conversation continues and subsequently,

Valentin makes a direct connection with "maleness" and violence:

>—[Valentin:] I don't know, but sometimes that kind of behavior can get in a man's way.
>—When? When it comes to torturing?
>—No, when it comes to being finished with the torturers.
>—But if men acted like women there wouldn't be any more torturers.
>—And you, what would you do without men?
>—You're right. They're mostly brutes, but I like them.
>—Molina . . . But you did say if they all acted like women then there wouldn't by any torturers. You've got a point there, a flimsy one, but still, it's a point.

Here we are confronted with a series of gender paradoxes and a clever deconstruction of male anxiety. I don't think Molina is necessarily making a biological argument that men will always act violently, because he himself has managed to re-gender himself. He wants men to "act like women," and he wants them to partake of the virtues that have been assigned to women, especially those of sensitivity and compassion. What becomes paradoxical is what Valentin points out, which is that Molina desires men, even though they're mostly "brutes." As will become clearer, Molina performs a type of gender transference. He continually identifies himself as a woman, but also makes the issue of gender between Valentin and himself more dynamic and less fixed.

It is also in this first section of the novel that their relationship is solidified through the movies, and this contributes to their comfort with gender play. When Molina expresses his sadness that the film will soon be finished, Valentin expresses his own sadness about it, and then a type of pact is made that the storytelling doesn't have to end:

>—[Molina speaking:] Tomorrow we'll be all finished with the film.
>—You don't know how sorry that makes me.
>—You too?
>—Yes, I'd like it to last a little longer. And the worst thing's that it's going to end sadly, Molina.
>—Well, it made the time go by faster, right?
>—But you didn't really really like it then.
>—Yes I did, and it's a shame to see it ending.
>—But don't be silly, I can tell you another one.
>—Honestly?
>—Sure, I remember lots of lovely, lovely films. (37)

This passage expresses how invested both of them are in the films and their importance in establishing and constructing their relationship.

A low-grade B picture such as *Cat People* has allowed them to share intimacies, to change identities, and to become closer linked. As we shall see, it is the texture of the films, and not always the specific narrative details that provide the environment for their "colic coupling." The film *Cat People* is essentially about transformations, and the fear, eroticism, and pleasure that can be gained by the unpredictability of its effects. It is placed deliberately at the start of the novel to set a tone of reception to various transformations. Things will be changing throughout the text, and just about every important category of identification becomes dislodged and dislocated from its "proper" meaning. What else gets set into motion is that Valentin becomes further drawn into the campy discourse that Molina instigates, a discourse that is usually about gender. When Valentin interrupts the movie because he is trying to "untangle a knot," of something important that he is thinking about, he claims he needs silence because "if you don't begin pulling the right thread . . . you'll lose it" (37). When they are going to sleep, Molina admonishes Valentin, "Don't lose that thread . . . But if you drop the ball of yarn, I'll give you zero in housekeeping, Miss Valentina." Valentin seems to take this in good stride, telling Molina not to "worry yourself about me . . . And don't call me Valentina, I'm no woman." Molina's good natured, campy and teasing response is, "How can I tell?" Valentin doesn't seem to mind this bantering and ends the exchange, with, "Sorry, Molina, but I don't give demonstrations . . . Good night, have a good sleep" (38). As we have seen before, to refer to men as "she" or "Miss" is part of gay male camping and slang. Molina deliberately uses this to tease Valentin about his masculinity, but also it expresses a closeness that is developing between them. "Miss Valentina" pokes fun not only at Valentin's masculinity but also involves him in Molina's camp discourse. By doing so, Valentin is denaturalized as a male subject, and even his type of revolutionary, serious maleness can be gently mocked by Molina's campiness. Molina himself, however, as seen in the torture discussion, is caught up in the contradictions of his own gendered perspective.

At one point, the two are discussing Valentin's revolutionary girlfriend and how they share a commitment to the struggle and against bourgeois morality. Valentin declares that "I don't believe in marriage— or in monogamy, to be more precise." Molina disagrees: "But how marvelous when a couple loves each other for a lifetime . . . It's my dream." Valentin then questions what he sees as the paradox, "So why do you like men then?" The rest of the exchange is as follows:

—[Molina speaking:] What's that got to do with it? . . . I'd like to marry a man for the rest of my life.

—So you're a regular bourgeois gentleman at heart, eh, Molina?
—Bourgeois lady, thank you.
—But don't you see how all that's nothing but a deception? If you were a woman, you wouldn't want that.
—I'm in love with a wonderful guy and all I ask is to live by his side for the rest of my life.
—And since that's impossible, because if he's a guy he wants a woman, well, you're never going to undeceive yourself. (44)

The bourgeois conventions that Valentin can see right through are instead taken as deeply felt aspirations for Molina. Like Venus Xtravaganza in *Paris is Burning*, Molina takes the bourgeoisie at its word: he does believe that if he were a woman he would find perfect contentment married to the man of his dreams, living a life of monogamous respectability. Valentin, however, doesn't believe that a "man" is capable of participating in that type of dream; he also doesn't think that a "man" will love Molina, since Molina isn't "really" a woman. But what would a camp reading make of Molina's dreams? We have seen that one definition of camp according to Newton's research is of incongruity. This incongruity, this type of "colic couplings" can begin to make sense of Molina's camp equations which don't neatly add up as "man + woman = love." The camp equation might be more like "man" + "woman" = "love." In other words, camp can suspend all assumptions about gender congruity, along with conventional assumptions about romance, even resolving unresolvable contradictions. Camp can allow a space for dreaming and having the impossible. All these dreams of gender transformation and transference, dreams that often take the aspect of camp, the dreams of contentment with a man someone loves, and the dreams of a political utopia in which all this would be possible becomes woven into the web of the novel.

The other movie I would like to discuss is a Nazi propaganda film that Molina remembers watching in Buenos Aires. He describes it in glowing terms, with a ravishing French heroine who is blackmailed by the sinister Resistance to betray her dashing German lover, who is trying to bring peace and prosperity to the world through Nazi occupation and extermination. The heroine is Leni, a beautiful, but lonely, cabaret singer who lives only for love and her singing. She is innocent of politics, and doesn't realize until it is too late how deeply implicated she is in intrigue. The plot also hinges on her lover's majordomo, who at the end, before she dies, is revealed to have been spying for the Resistance all along. World War II Europe, treachery, blackmail, sexy Parisian cabarets, dashing blonde men, disfigured villains, and a gorgeous woman caught in the middle of it all: this film clearly captures Molina's full imagination.

He describes one scene in which Leni is being romanced by the German officer in his beautiful home outside of Paris. They are listening to music, music that fills the German with intense emotion, claiming the violins "are like the waters of a German river, navigated by some man-god who actually is just a man, but whose love of country makes him invincible, like a god, because now he knows no fear whatsoever." This reference to the "man-god" is obviously Hitler, and the officer is so moved he cries. This is precisely, in turn, what moves Molina so deeply, since he loves the display of sensitivity on the part of the authoritarian officer: "And that's what's so marvelous about the scene now, because seeing how moved he is, she realizes how much he too has his emotions like any man, even though he seems invincible as a god" (55). Molina is identifying with Leni and sharing the feelings she would have toward such an intense display of masculine emotion. That the man is deeply moved by the idea of the Nation, and not necessarily by feelings of romance is not important to Leni/Molina and the sentimentality behind the glory of the nation displayed here by a Nazi does not deter Molina from his adulation of the scene. He then describes in great detail the particulars of the shot when Leni realizes she is in love, and I quote the passage in its entirety for several reasons. While Molina often describes scenes from the movies he narrates in full detail, in this instance he uses precise language to paint a vivid portrait in shades of grey. The scene is also described only in terms of visual display and sentiment. Molina elides the context within which this display of aesthetic sentimentality takes place:

> He tries to conceal his feelings by going over to the window. A full moon's over the city of Paris, the grounds around the house seem silvery, black trees set against the gray sky, not blue, because the film's in black and white. The white fountain bordered by jasmine, flowers in silvery-white too, and the camera on her face then with a close-up, all in divine grays, with perfect shadowing, and a tear rolling down her cheek. When it's just about to fall it's not so shiny, but when it starts to run down along her high cheekbone the tear begins to shine as much as the diamonds in her necklace. And the camera again shows you the silvery garden, and there you are in the movies but it's more as if you were a bird taking off because now you see the garden from above, smaller and smaller . . . (56–57)

This is one of Molina's most cinematically self-reflexive passages. He describes the scene in strong photographic terms and even calls attention to the cinematic technique only to disclaim the reality of the technology of cinema. This is the one film in which Molina seems to get the most aesthetically lost. The close descriptions suggest the great and lasting impression it has made upon him. Immediately after relating this scene, he asks Valentin what he thinks:

—Do you like the picture?
—I don't know yet. And you, why do you like it so much? You seem transported.
—If I had the chance to choose one film to see all over again, it would have to be this one. (56)

Molina is indeed "transported." The film has had such an intense effect on him that he is able to be aware of it as a film, and yet practically begin to live within the film itself. What is it that strikes Molina so much about this Nazi film? No other scene from this film will be related in such loving detail. Leni's close-up with a silver tear is not just a cliché from "old movies," it is the romance of film itself, that can offer up the smallest intimate moment into a gigantic close-up. Leni's tears sparking like diamonds are shed for a Nazi, and it doesn't take a Valentin to see the darker motives of this film that Molina loves so much:

—[Valentin speaking:] But why? It's a piece of Nazi junk, or don't you realize . . .
—No, it's that if there's any junk around here it might be you and not the film. So don't speak to me anymore . . . Of course you're offensive the way you . . . you think I don't even . . . realize what Nazi propa— . . . ganda is, but even If I . . . if I do like it, well, that's be— . . . because it's well made, and besides it's a work of art, you don't under— . . . understand because you never even saw it.
—But you must be crazy, crying over that! (56)

Molina has been able to transform a piece of "Nazi junk" into a fantasy film, filled with beauty and romance. This power of transformation is surely suspect and captures the essence of the problem of representation and reception. Can various elements of expressive culture which seem self-defeating and contaminated with commodified sentimentality in fact be powerful modes of affective resistance? May they contain elements of "truth" essential to any political struggle? Is there finally any mode of culture that is ultimately not recoupable? If Molina prizes a Nazi film for its display of emotion, and he empowers himself through these images, does that finally redeem the film itself?

It is as if Puig himself is calling into question his own project of redeeming the "junk" of mass culture—the "deception" of mass culture that critics on the right and the left warn us about. But what does it mean to evacuate a Nazi propaganda film of its propaganda? Molina here is demonstrating a powerful means of "reading," in which he is able to ignore the blatant fascism of the filmmakers. It may be that this ability to ignore the strongest, most oppressive mechanisms in order to retrieve what is necessary for survival is what has served Molina well, even though he is in prison. In fact, what makes Molina so sentimental and weepy when describing the film, is that it reminds him of Gabriel, his obsession on the "outside."

Molina tells Valentin that Gabriel is a waiter, who is "marvelous looking . . . very intelligent, but he had none of the opportunities in life, and here he is still working at that shitty job, but he deserves so much more. Which makes me feel like I want to help him out" (57). Molina admits that Gabriel is "completely straight. I was the one who started it all" (58). As if to signal that Molina's love for Gabriel signifies something about Puig's view of homosexuality, Valentin presses Molina for detail, expressing that, "I think I have to know more about you, that's what, in order to understand you better. If we're going to be in this cell together like this, we ought to understand one another better, and I know very little about people with your type of inclination" (59). It is also at this point in the text, that Puig begins his famous footnotes that detail the scientific and psychoanalytic debates about the origins of homosexuality.

Molina agrees to tell him his story, but not to reveal Gabriel's name, and when telling the story, Molina refers to himself as a woman, because "when it comes to him I can't talk about myself like a man, because I don't feel like one" (60). Molina goes to the restaurant daily to watch Gabriel's movements which he describes as "powerful . . . so elegant, and soft, and masculine at the same time." Here Valentin presses him to explain his definition of masculinity, which Molina does: "It's a lot of things, but for me . . . well, the nicest thing about a man is just that, to be marvelous-looking, and strong, but without making any fuss about it, and also walking very tall. Walking absolutely straight, like my waiter, who's not afraid to say anything. And it's knowing what you want, where you're going." At this, Valentin pronounces unknowingly the final verdict on the construction of masculinity, "That's pure fantasy, that type doesn't exist" (61). This leads to a testy argument between them, until Molina finally asks Valentin what he thinks a "man" is. Valentin is caught a bit unawares, but offers this: "Mmm . . . his not taking any crap . . . from anyone, not even the powers that be . . . But no, it's more than that. Not taking any crap is one thing, but not the most important. What really makes a man is a lot more, it has to do with not humiliating someone else with an order, or a tip. Even more, it's . . . not letting the person next to you feel degraded, feel bad" (63). Molina, in turn, skeptically remarks that Valentin has described a "saint." Each of their descriptions of what they believe a "man" to be is instantly met by the other with disbelief that this "man" exists. This serves to erode commonsensical ideas about what exactly a "man" is. In fact, both Molina and Valentin have their own fantasies about "men," fantasies that they both cannot live without.

Molina goes on describing his love for Gabriel, how he eventually convinced him to have coffee with him, and how he found out details about his life. Gabriel had started off playing professional soccer, but when he saw the rampant corruption around, he refused to play the game, "because the guy's straight that way, too." He eventually quits soccer and starts working at a factory, a job that his somewhat wealthy fiancée arranged for him. He marries the woman and almost immediately gets promoted to foreman. But at the factory he took the union side in a labor dispute and ended up quitting. He was then unemployed until he found a job waiting tables, which is where he met Molina. Gabriel's sad story makes Molina "love him all the more," but he becomes distressed because Gabriel "wouldn't let me do anything for him." The fact is that Gabriel has a wife, but Molina admits "deep down I hated everything about her. Just the thought of him sleeping next to her every night made me die of jealousy" (68). Molina admits that nothing ever happened sexually between them, and that "there was no convincing him on that score." At one point Gabriel is fighting a lot with his wife and Molina lets himself think that he might have a chance if they break up. But when he asks Gabriel if he would like a pair of pajamas for Father's Day, there is a "complete disaster." Valentin, engaged in the story, says, "Don't leave me hanging," and Molina reveals that Gabriel didn't need pajamas, since he "always slept in the raw . . . It killed me." Molina relates how he had "such illusions." He then describes exactly what those illusions were:

> I wanted to convince him there was still a chance for him to go back to school and get a degree or something . . . That he might come to live with me, with my mom and me. And I'd help him, and make him study. And not bother about anything but him, the whole blessed day, getting everything all set for him, his clothes, buying his books, registering him for courses, and little by little I'd convince him that what he had to do was just one thing: never work again. And I'd pass along whatever small

amount of money was needed to give the wife for child support, and make him not worry about anything at all, nothing except himself, until he got what he wanted and lost all that sadness of his for good, wouldn't that be marvelous? (69)

Molina describes his dream of love as consisting of completely living for someone else's happiness. This kind of selfless care is a form of transformation: Molina is able to transform himself into a servile role, one conventionally relegated and resisted by women, just for his lover, because to care for someone else is the highest and noblest form of existence. He does not want an egalitarian relationship at all. He wants nothing but for his man to have no thought for anything but himself. The illusions Molina has do not just concern his love for a straight man or that he is a woman, but also that he can exist only for, and through, someone else. He is transforming what a "self" is. He is also, in the process, still transforming Valentin's relationship with camp, in which camp can function as a metamorphosis.

When they say goodnight to each other after this story, Valentin admits that he will probably stay up later: "See how life is, Molina, here I am staying up at night, thinking about your boyfriend" (71). In the middle of one of Molina's detailed narrations of a scene in the Nazi film that takes place in a garden that Molina describes as a French, Valentin corrects by claiming the garden is "German . . . Saxon to be exact . . . Because the French gardens use lots of flowers, and even though the arrangements are geometrical they tend to be much more casual looking. The garden sounds German." To this Molina campily replies, "One of these days they'll realize who's the fag around here" (77). It is also in this section of the novel that the torture device of poisoned food occurs. The prison guards have poisoned one of the dishes, and in this instance, Molina eats it. It will later be revealed to have been a mistake, as it was intended for Valentin, so that he would be weakened enough to reveal information to Molina. But when Molina is attacked with severe cramps, he still manages to use camp, and Valentin learns how to read it. Molina is in such pain from the poison that Valentin tells him to continue telling the Nazi film, so that he won't think about the pain. (88) When Molina does, he narrates a part where the maquis, or the Resistance, are vilified in the film. Valentin asks him, "Yes, but you know the maquis were actually heroes, don't you?" Molina then gives a camp answer: "Hey, what do you take me for, an even dumber broad than I am?" Valentin is then able to read Molina's campiness as a good sign about his health: "If you're into that girl stuff again you must be feeling better" (89). It is instances such as this that show a greater awareness on Valentin's part about Molina's campiness. It also shows a growing connection between the two, as they share even more about their lives.

The Nazi film is important because it shows the amount of "reality" that Molina can shut out. He is able to respond to the film, and to different situations in his life, in ways that bring him pleasure or comfort. Valentin is impatient with this type of comfort, because he sees it as deluded and reactionary. Molina's story of Gabriel displays his romantic idealism, and his ability to invest impractical or impossible situations with hope. But it also reveals his wanting to become self-less. He is willing to give himself up to a man, because that is how he will feel most like "himself." In this sense he sees himself as a "woman," who is looking for a "man" who will allow him to do this. He is in a sense looking for an illusion, albeit a campy one. When the poisoning begins, though, Valentin at once acknowledges the importance of distraction and of illusion to alleviate pain.

"We're Normal Women, We Sleep with Men"

Later, when Valentin is racked with pain due to the poison, he confides in Molina the real story of his own true love. Valentin admits that before he "was putting you on about my girlfriend. The one I told you about is someone else, who I loved very much" (130). Molina begs him not to tell him any confidential information, telling him he fears he might be interrogated. Valentin discounts this, asking him, "who would ask you something about me, about my goings-on?" (131). Molina manages to distract him with a cup of tea, but in the next scene he is singing a bolero to himself, one that he says is called "My Letter." While Valentin says it sounds like "a lot of romantic nonsense," Molina defends himself with, "I happen to like boleros, and that one's really very pretty. I'm sorry if it wasn't very tactful, though" (133). He is referring to the fact that Valentin had received a letter that day that had left him looking depressed. Valentin shares the letter, which is from his revolutionary girlfriend. It is written in a type of code in which she informs Valentin the activities and setbacks of the group.

Reading the letter to Molina, Valentin realizes that the letter had left him feeling the way Molina's bolero described the singer feeling about a letter, "There I was laughing at your bolero, but the letter I got today says just what the bolero says . . . It seems to me I don't have any right to be laughing at your bolero." He asks Molina to sing the bolero again for him: "Dearest . . . I am writing you once more now, night . . . brings a silence that helps me talk to you, and I wonder . . . could you be remembering too, sad dreams . . . of this strange love affair. My dear . . . although life may never let us meet again, and we—because of fate—must always live apart . . . I swear, this heart of mine will be always yours . . . my thoughts, my whole life, forever yours . . . just as this pain . . . belongs . . . to you . . ." (137). Molina describes the bolero as "divine," It is that very bolero that moves Valentin to tell the truth about the woman he really loves, who he met in the movement, but after they fell in love she quit and demanded he do the same. Valentin refused, and she began interfering with his activities. This was the last straw, and they separated. Valentin has not seen her for two years, but admits that he still "thinks about her . . . it seems like we were destined to be separated." At this Molina adds, "Because you loved each other too much?" Valentin sees the sentiment behind this and tells him, "That sounds like another bolero, Molina." Molina knows the value of such sentiments, however, and tells him, "Listen, big man, don't you know by now, boleros contain tremendous truths, which is why I like them" (139). The "tremendous truth" is that Valentin himself suffers from love, and has also participated in the romance of an impossible love. He allowed political circumstances to separate him from his lover, but he regrets it and suffers for it. He is also disgusted with himself for loving Marta, because, as he says, "I don't feel attracted to her for any good reasons, but because . . . she has class . . . that's right, class, just like the class-conscious pigs would say . . . in their son-of-a-bitching world" (145). Valentin tells this story as he is wrenched by cramps from the poisoned food, and once again Molina cleans up after him and fixes him a clean fresh bed. Valentin cries out of sorrow and frustration, and the two are woven closer together.

It is at this point that it is revealed to the reader that Molina has been under orders to discover information about Valentin. He is told that his mother has been notified that he may be released early, and her health has already improved due to the good news. Molina is being drawn in tighter and tighter, since it is clear that now he has begun to develop feelings for Valentin, and betraying him will not be so simple. To cover up the true purpose of the meeting, the prison officials suggest that they provide groceries that Molina can claim his mother brought him in a visit. Molina gives them a list of provisions that his mother would most likely have brought him. Molina returns to the cell with his groceries and shares them with Valentin. The sharing of the groceries brings them together even closer, and after a decent meal, Valentin suggests:

> —Because there is one thing that's still lacking to complete the usual program.
> —Christ, and I'm the one who's supposed to be degenerate here.
> —No, no kidding. We should have a film now, that's what's missing... Do you remember any others like the panther woman? That's the one I like best.
> —Well sure, I know lots of supernatural ones... And there's one about a zombie woman...
> —That's it! That sounds terrific! (157)

And so the web is almost complete. Valentin is now completely complicit in a relationship with Molina. They both enjoy the pleasures of nice food, provided by the terrorist state, and are ready for the escape of a movie.

In the middle of telling another film, Valentin has a violent outburst and throws the hot plate at Molina. He is filled with remorse, saying that he has acted like a "real bastard." When they are making up, Valentin makes his point about the cell being a type of island away from repression, where they can create their own world. Molina is touched and tells Valentin: "I respect you, and I'm fond of you, and I want you to feel the same way about me, too..." When Valentin asks him whether or not he has close friends, Molina replies:

> Yes, but look, my friends have always been... well, faggots like I am, and among ourselves, well, how can I put it? We don't put too much faith in one another, because of the way we are... so easy to scare, so wishy-washy. And what we're always waiting for... is like a friendship or something, with a more serious person... with a man, of course. And that can't happen, because a man... what he wants is a woman... there's the other kind [homosexuals] who fall in love with one another. But as for my friends and myself, we're a hundred percent female. We don't go in for those little games—that's strictly for homos. We're normal women; we sleep with men. (203)

Molina's ideas about true love then seem to involve two factors: A straight "real" man and a complete disavowal of self. This ability to give up oneself, he identifies as being a "true" woman in love. Molina admits that what he and his friends are waiting for can't happen, and yet it's what they wait for, despite all the odds against it. Falling in love with a straight man, or rather, falling in love with a man is like one of the movies Molina narrates. You get to design it and have as many illusions about it as you like, since it becomes your story, your movie. The imagination can conjure up any number of scenarios—even if the scenario is overdetermined from the start. In this case it is overdetermined by the constraints of gender.

Metamorphosis

What Molina can imagine is both inside and outside of a heterosexual and homosexual economy. If what he wants is a conventional romance, it must consist of a man and a woman. He wants the gender roles to be clearly demarcated. This involves a reimagining of "marriage" and "gender" to the point of parody. Molina is taking heterosexuality at its word, and somehow he reformulates and transforms (in a type of colic coupling), the traditional in a radically creative way. He doesn't consider himself "homosexual" per se; he claims not to go for those "little games," that he is "a hundred percent female." It is clear that he is not a "hundred percent female," but that instead he is exercising camp and drag vocabulary in order to map out his desires. Molina cannot imagine himself with another gay man, partly because he sees other gay men as being like him, as being feminine-identified. Molina has left the heterosexual and homosexual economies in order to follow the trajectory of gender.

It would be fairly easy and even reductive to describe what Molina ultimately wants as a version of male homosexual patriarchy, with its overemphasis on masculinity and conventional role-playing, and that very well may be the case. But I think it may be more useful to think of Judith Butler's argument in a discussion on drag of how the "presence of so-called heterosexual conventions within homosexual contexts as well as the proliferation of specifically gay discourses of sexual difference . . . cannot be explained as chimerical representations of originally heterosexual identities. And neither can they be understood as the pernicious insistence of heterosexist constructs within gay sexuality and identity . . . The replication of heterosexual constructs in non-heterosexual frames brings into relief the utterly constructed status of the so-called heterosexual original" (111). Molina is not simply attempting to replicate a conventional marriage, or attempting to be a conventional woman, he is redesigning the terms on which these are established in contemporary society. A clue that he is refashioning these terms is his engagement with camp. His drawing upon elements of camp and humor signify that he knows what he is doing. This is not to say that he doesn't "really" consider himself a woman, or that he doesn't "really" want a man, but that these desires are mediated by camp.

His insistence on playing the "woman" may also be tied to his concept of being gay as being a type of woman. Anthropologist Stephen O. Murray in his article "Machismo, Male Homosexuality, and Latino Culture" (collected in his book, *Latin American Male Homosexualities*) argues that:

> The former Iberian colonies in the New World provide the most often described example of the gender-defined organization of homosexuality. Across a number of Caribbean, South, and Mesoamerican culture areas . . . ideal (cultural) norms distinguish masculine inserters (*activos*) who are not considered homosexuals from feminine insertees (*pasivos*) who are. The queen as vividly represented in the work of the Argentine writer Manuel Puig, has accepted and bowed to the macho ethic, abandoned the impossible and forbidden partial masculinity of bisexuality, and become a woman—a fallen one at that . . . the clear and simple masculine/feminine division is paramount in Latino views of gender and sex . . . (50; 63)

Murray contends that in Latino culture, the *pasivo* becomes a type of woman, exactly what Molina would contend. In Puig's own terminology, Molina is a queen, more than a woman, and yet somewhat less. "Queen" itself, in addition, carries camp connotations, suggesting a failed type of royalty and authority.

The *pasivo/activo* divide is important in the text, because it is at this point that Molina reveals that he will be released in a few days. When he becomes distraught, Valentin begins to comfort him by rubbing his back, and giving him comforting words. The following passage then suggests that they have anal sex. Molina is the passive partner in sex, fulfilling what it is that he wanted. He is having sex with a dominant man who will make him feel like a "woman," since Valentin is "straight." But what happens next suspends all of these notions at least temporarily. Molina describes how, "Just then, without thinking, I put my hand up to my face, trying to find the mole." Valentin reminds him that he has a mole, not Molina. He agrees, but insists, "I know. But I put my hand to my forehead, to feel the mole that . . . I haven't got." Molina goes on to exclaim that, "And know what else I felt, Valentin? But only for a second, no more . . . For just a second, it seemed like I wasn't here . . . not here or anywhere out there either . . . It seemed as if I wasn't here at all . . . like it was you all alone . . . Or like I wasn't me anymore. As if now, somehow . . . I . . . were you" (219). The transformation is complete: Molina has now "become" Valentin, but does this mean that he has now become a "man"? The paradox involved here confuses the gender framework that Molina has set up. The unexpected has occurred.

Valentin, too, has undergone a transformation, although his is illustrated differently. The morning after they make love, Molina tells Valentin that "I think I haven't felt so happy since when I was a kid. Since when my mom used to buy me a toy, or something like that." Valentin for some reason becomes curious, and asks Molina to tell him, "I want to know if you remember a toy you even liked most of all . . . of all the toys your mother bought you." Molina's answer: "A dolly." Valentin bursts into laughter, "I wanted to see if there was any relation between myself and that toy . . ." He presses Molina, half jokingly, "You're sure it wasn't like a toy soldier or something like that?" Molina is quite precise: "No a dolly with very blond hair, all braided up, and she could blink her eyes, and wore a Bavarian costume." Valentin cannot stop laughing, and Molina claims, "I swear I never saw you laugh before" (223). The laughter that fills Valentin is perhaps his recognition that he too has been dramatically transformed. He is perhaps like Molina's favorite toy, a dolly. That he laughs signifies his own final participation in Molina's campiness.

Of course, their brief affair ends sadly. Molina is released from prison, after promising Valentin that he will pass on information. He at first refused to do so, but everything changes when he asks Valentin for a kiss. He asks, "I'm curious would you feel much revulsion about giving me a kiss?" Valentin replies, "It must be a fear that you'll turn into a panther, like with the first movie you told me." Molina protests that he's not the panther woman, and Valentin agrees, telling him that, "You, you're the spider woman, that traps men in her web" (260). But they both are now trapped in a web of desire—one of their own making. This kiss is the transformation that the book has been wanting to perform: the transformation of the grimmest possible conditions into a utopia. If Foucault is right that power is always productive, in this case, power has produced what Molina has always dreamed of, and that may be what the novel has been all along—a dream—a dream that Molina has dreamed even in the worst of material circumstances.

That Molina's attempts for love end in pain is actually part of his "script," and part of his "reading" of melodramatic movies. Representations of unrequited and/or doomed love contain a poignancy because they are reminders of the regulatory regimes we live under. They are not masochistic or self-defeating desires to be hurt, but a political recognition that "true" happiness and love may be impossible at this historical moment. But it is this "may be impossible" that is so important, because it holds out the possibility of change: the possibility of something completely different. The campy language of *The Boys in the Band*, the melancholy closet of Arturo Islas, the utopian aspirations of drag, and the love of movies and gender play of Molina, all ache for something better—over the rainbow, perhaps, but worth fighting for, or at least imagining, for now.

Conclusion: *Somewhere Better Than This Place/Nowhere Better Than This Place*

In 1990, artist Felix Gonzalez-Torres exhibited two large white stacks of paper at the Andrea Rosen Gallery in New York City. These stacks consisted of sheets of paper measuring 29 inches by 23 inches, and the artist directed that the stacks be endlessly replenished, as viewers were encouraged to take sheets of the paper home with them. On the center of the sheets in one pile was printed: "Somewhere Better Than This Place." The twin stack read: "Nowhere Better Than This Place." The stacks looked like large white cubes, referencing the monumental and spare sculpture of Minimalism, while slyly parodying its permanence. The work also drew from Conceptual Art, in which the *idea* of the artwork, as opposed to its visual manifestation, is paramount. Gonzalez-Torres actively required the viewer to respond to this "idea" and to shatter the sacrosanct space between the object and the spectator. The gallery visitor was invited to take something—not just a souvenir, but the artwork itself. Here, Gonzalez-Torres remakes the relationship between buyer and seller, between artist and viewer, and interrupts, however briefly, the steady exchange of consumer goods.

Gonzalez-Torres had directed his artistic output by this time toward two different forms he described as "stacks" and "spills." Spills usually consisted of piles of candy, carefully weighed and placed in the corner of a gallery. For example, one artwork, "Untitled" (Lover Boys) contained exactly 355 pounds of candy individually wrapped in silver cellophane. The weight Gonzalez-Torres specified was the combined weight of his lover and himself. Viewers were to take away as much candy as they liked.

What is the viewer taking away in artworks such as these? Gonzalez-Torres' lover died of AIDS in 1991, and the weight of the candies is the total of the two lovers' *healthy* weights. Each candy taken diminishes the weight of the spill, and each piece incarnates the two "lover boys" into a sweet edible form. But like the stacks, the candy spills are endlessly replenished, so there is no end, no finality, no death. A full scale retrospective of Gonzalez-Torres' work filled the Guggenheim Museum in 1995, where viewers left with tubes filled with sheets of paper and pockets filled with candies. In 1996, the artist died of AIDS.

I choose to talk about the white paper stacks—the formal title of the artwork is "Untitled"—because they represent the portable accessibility of utopian possibilities through the distribution and impact of these sheets into the culture at large. Where is there "somewhere better than this place"? Gonzalez-Torres created the stacks to "celebrate the notion of the here and now as a moment to envision." Here the artist describes his work:

> As with all artistic practices, my work is related to the act of leaving one place for another, one which proves perhaps better than the first . . . Traveling is also about dying . . . It is, after all, about death . . . When I went to Paris for the first time, I had already been there thousands of times. I had been to Paris because I dreamt about going there with Ross and walking down the Champs-Élysées and going to the Louvre. When I finally was in Paris, it was just to bring my physical entity, my body, there as a completion of what I had dreamt before. And when that happens, that is real traveling. (81)

The idea of travel here encompasses both physical and psychic distances, and one is not privileged over the other. The large blank space of the sheet of paper serves as a type of movie screen to project inner desires, with the wording suggesting both public and private spheres. Is this "place" part of a physical geography or is it an emotionally occupied space, a potential shift in consciousness?

The ability to imagine something better is here coupled with the inability to imagine "nowhere better than this place." Affirmatively, this statement can refer to being blissfully present in a moment that could not get any better. It can also be read as despairing and bitter, a recognition that there is nowhere better to go. Gonzalez-Torres requires the viewer to participate not only in creating meaning but also in changing or determining meaning. This ability to imagine is important because it stands in the face of loss and hopelessness. The white sheets are emptied of visual stimuli, but we are required to fill them up (or not):

> This work originated from my fear of losing everything. This work is about controlling my own fear. My work cannot be destroyed. I have

destroyed it already, from day one. The feeling is almost like when you are in a relationship with someone and you know it's not going to work out. From the very beginning, you know that you don't really have to worry about it not working out because you simply know that it won't. The person then cannot abandon you, because he has already abandoned you from day one—that is how I made this work. That is why I made this work. This work cannot disappear. This work cannot be destroyed the same way other things in my life have disappeared and have left me. I destroyed it myself instead. I had control over it and this what has empowered me. But it is a very masochistic kind of power. I destroy the work before I make it. (122)

The utopian yearnings of Gonzalez-Torres' work come out of loss and despair. It is this paradox of finding power in powerlessness, of finding art in junk, and of thinking about the presence of utopia in the state of loss that has guided this project.

The first text I chose to highlight this is Mart Crowley's *The Boys in the Band* because I am drawn to the tension in the play and also to its incessant references to Hollywood movies and actresses. The play captures the spirit of pre-Stonewall gay male urban culture, including its less appealing aspects. Part of its disrepute lies in the characters' self-loathing and their perpetual inability to find lasting, stable love. One of the characters in the play is African-American and his marginality contributes to his experience with unrequited love: he has never forgotten his love for the white son of his mother's employer. However, both wounded characters in Crowley's play confront emotional devastation fearlessly and ultimately provide comfort to each other.

Turning to Sandra Cisneros' short story "Bien Pretty" and Arturo Islas' novel *Migrant Souls* I explored the relationship of popular culture and romantic sentiment to suffering, within a Chicana/o context. In the short story, the main character, Lupe, falls madly in love with Flavio, an exterminator. Lupe is highly educated, Flavio is not, and the story explores how the relationship, based on desire for cultural authenticity, builds to sexual fulfillment, and eventually, romantic disappointment. When Lupe nurses her broken heart, she finds unexpected solace and empowerment from the heroines of Latina love found in *telenovelas*.

Miguel Chico, the main character in Islas' novel, closely resembles the author himself, in biographical and emotional detail. The novel explores his family's attachment to suffering, beginning with the matriarch, Mama Chona, crossing the border into the United States. Miguel Chico and his cousin, Josie, while growing up, invented a secret society—Our Lady of Perpetual Suffering—to whom they make offerings when undergoing emotional strife. Islas explores the connection between suffering and Chicano identity in ways that bring together Catholicism, Hollywood movies, and the practice of writing itself. The novel has a melancholic tone, which suits its content perfectly; I contend, however, that this tone contains its own element of hope and faith in love.

While desire functions in these texts as a forward and romantic movement toward the love object (however futile), through drag, I also want to think about desire as a movement consisting of ambition and of longing for stardom, glamour, and escape. The theme of a drag as yearning for a better place arises from two examples—one the instance of Judy Garland and her imitators and the other is *Paris is Burning*. In both of these cases, there is a drive toward recognition and the spotlight. But they are also marked by extreme suffering and eventual loss. Instead of believing that these are participants in a theatrical glorification of suffering (which admittedly in many senses they are) I argue that drag contains utopian desires of creating something valuable from abjection.

Manuel Puig's novel *Kiss of the Spider Woman* contains perhaps the grandest representation of affirmation through abjection in the persona of Molina, who shares a close and campy kinship with *The Boys in the Band*. Molina's ability to find utopian solace in crass Hollywood narratives is counterpoised with his cellmate Valentin's stern Marxist analyses, which read the movies quite poorly. Puig poses the question of whether popular culture contains utopian narratives that can combat even physical torture. His book addresses complicated issues such as these and eventually redefines the questions themselves.

Richard Dyer, in an essay on disco, reads Diana Ross' "Touch Me in the Morning" as expressing the "intensity of fleeting emotional contacts . . . which have built in them the recognition of the (inevitably) temporary quality of the experience." He claims that this aspect of disco's "romanticism provides an embodiment and validation of an aspect of gay culture." Dyer sees the passion and intensity of this romanticism as offering:

> a glimpse of what it means to live at the height of our emotional and experiential capacities—not dragged down by the banality of organized routine life. Given that everyday banality, work, domesticity, ordinary sexism and racism, are rooted in the structures of class and gender of this society, the flight from that banality can be seen as—is—a flight from capitalism and patriarchy themselves as lived experiences. (155–156)

If the emotions expressed in popular, literary, and expressive culture seem to always describe a love that has either soured or a love that is pitched so high as to be out of reach, then at the same time, these expressions provide a utopian ideal of emotional and even social transformation. If we lived in a different, better sort of world, these texts imply, perhaps we could have a decent go at it. The loss and lament of AIDS also echoes through this book since creative figures who influenced it—Islas, Puig, Gonzalez-Torres—died of AIDS-related causes. Their physical absence, as gay Latinos, strikes a deep chord in my writing here. What to do with all this loss was a central compelling mystery for me. I hope to bring something to these losses of history, of culture— a sense that the historical memory embedded in these different forms of art can take us "somewhere better than this place."

REFERENCES

Films Cited

All About Eve. D., Joseph L. Mankiewicz. 1950.
All This, and Heaven Too. D., Anatole Litvak. 1940.
Annie Hall. D., Woody Allen. 1977.
Baby Face. D., Alfred E. Green. 1933.
Bicycle Thieves. D., Vittorio de Sica. 1947.
Blade Runner. D., Ridley Scott. 1982.
Breathless. D., Jean-Luc Godard. 1959.
Broadway Melody of 1938. D., Roy Del Ruth. 1937.
Camille. D., George Cukor. 1937.
Cape Fear. D., Martin Scorsese. 1991.
Casablanca. D., Michael Curtiz. 1942.
Cat on a Hot Tin Roof. D., Richard Brooks. 1958.
Cat People. D., Jacques Tourneur. 1942.
A Clockwork Orange. D., Stanley Kubrick. 1971.
Commando. D., Mark L. Lester. 1985.
Coney Island. D., Walter Lang. 1943.
The Devil and Miss Jones. D., Sam Wood. 1941.
Discreet Charm of the Bourgeoisie. D., Luis Buñuel. 1972.
Dolly Sisters. D., Irving Cummings. 1945.
Earth. D., Alexander Dovzhenko. 1930.
The Enchanted Cottage. D., John Cromwell. 1945.
Eraserhead. D., David Lynch. 1978.
The Exterminating Angel. D., Luis Buñuel. 1962.
The Four-Hundred Blows. D., Francois Truffaut. 1959.
The Gold Diggers of 1933. D., Mervyn LeRoy. 1933.
The Graduate. D., Mike Nichols. 1967.
The Great Lie. D., Edmund Goulding. 1941.
Guys and Dolls. D., Joseph L. Mankiewicz. 1955.
His Girl Friday. D., Howard Hawks. 1940.
I Walked With a Zombie. D., Jacques Tourneur. 1943.
Jules et Jim. D., Francois Truffaut. 1961.
Kiss Me Kate. D., George Sidney. 1953.
The Lady Eve. D., Preston Sturges. 1941.
L'Age D'Or. D., Luis Buñuel. 1930.

Las Vampiras. D., Frederico Curiel. 1969.
The Letter. D., William Wyler. 1940.
Love and Death. D., Woody Allen. 1975.
Meet Me in St. Louis. D., Vincente Minnelli. 1944.
The More the Merrier. D., George Stevens. 1943.
Mother. D., Vsvolod I. Pudovkin. 1926.
My Man Godfrey. D., Gregory La Cava. 1936.
A Night at the Opera. D., Sam Wood. 1935.
The Pirate. D., Vincente Minnelli. 1948.
Pufnstuf. D., Hollingsworth Morse. 1970.
The Return of the Jedi. D., Richard Marquand. 1983.
Singin' in the Rain. D., Gene Kelly, Stanley Donen. 1952.
A Star is Born. D., George Cukor. 1954.
Stella Dallas. D., King Vidor. 1937.
St. Elmo's Fire. D., Joel Schumacher. 1985.
A Streetcar Named Desire. D., Elia Kazan. 1951.
Suddenly, Last Summer. D., Joseph L. Mankiewicz. 1959.
Summer and Smoke. D., Peter Glenville. 1961.
Sweet Bird of Youth. D., Richard Brooks. 1962.
The Texas Chainsaw Massacre, Part III. D., Kim Henkel. 1997.
Top Hat. D., Mark Sandrich. 1935.
Un Chien Andalou. D., Luis Buñuel. 1929.
Wabash Avenue. D., Henry Kostser. 1950.
Weekend. D., Jean-Luc Godard. 1967.
West Side Story. D., Robert Wise, Jerome Robbins. 1962.
Whatever Happened to Baby Jane? D., Robert Aldrich. 1962.
The Wizard of Oz. D., Victor Fleming. 1939.
The Women. D., George Cukor. 1939.

Works Cited

Ahmed, Aijaz. *In Theory: Classes, Nations, Literatures.* New York: Verso, 1992.
Albee, Edward. *Who's Afraid of Virginia Woolf?* New York: Pocket Books, 1962.
Almaguer, Tomas. "Chicano Men: A Cartography of Homosexual Identity and Behavior." *Differences: A Journal of Feminist Cultural Studies.* Vol. 3, No. 2 (1991).
"April In Paris." E. Y. Harburg and Vernon Duke.
Anzaldua, Gloria. *Borderlands/La Frontera: The New Mestiza.* San Francisco: Spinsters/Aunt Lute, 1987.
As The World Turns. CBS-TV.
Bacarisse, Pamela. *The Necessary Dream: A Study of the Novels of Manuel Puig.* Cardiff: University of Wales Press, 1988.
Berten, Hans. *The Idea of the Postmodern: A History.* New York: Routledge, 1995.
Bronski, Michael. *Culture Clash: The Making of Gay Sensibility.* Boston: South End Press, 1984.

Brooks, Peter. *Reading for the Plot: Design and Interpretation in Narrative.* New York: A. A. Knopf, 1984.
Butler, Judith. *Gender Trouble: Feminism and the Subversion of Identity.* New York: Routledge, 1990.
Butler, Judith. *Bodies that Matter: On the Discursive Limits of "Sex".* New York: Routledge, 1993.
Carrier, Joseph. *De Los Otros: Intimacy and Homosexuality Among Mexican Men.* New York: Columbia University Press, 1995.
Champagne, John. *The Ethics of Marginality: A New Approach to Gay Studies.* Minneapolis: University of Minnesota Press, 1995.
Cisneros, Sandra. *Woman Hollering Creek and Other Stories.* New York: Random House, 1991.
Clurman, Harold. *The Collected Works of Harold Clurman: Six Decades of Commentary on Theatre, Dance, Music, Film, Arts and Letters.* New York: Applause Theatre Books Publication, 1993.
Colas, Santiago. *Postmodernity in Latin America: The Argentine Paradigm.* Durham: Duke University Press, 1994.
Core, Philip. *Camp: The Lie that tells the Truth.* London: Plexus Publishing, 1984.
Crowley, Mart. *The Boys in the Band.* New York: Samuel French, Inc., 1968.
Diaz, Rafael M. *Latino Gay Men: Culture, Sexuality, and Risk Behavior.* New York: Routledge, 1998.
Doty, Alexander. *Making Things Perfectly Queer: Interpreting Mass Culture.* Minneapolis: University of Minnesota Press, 1993.
Drinnon, Richard. *Facing West: The Metaphysics of Indian-Hating and Empire Building.* New York: Schocken Books, 1990.
Dyer, Richard. *Heavenly Bodies: Film Stars and Society.* London: The MacMillan Press LTD, 1986.
Dyer, Richard. *Only Entertainment.* New York: Routledge, 1992.
Dyer, Richard. *The Matter of Images: Essays on Representation.* New York: Routledge, 1993.
Fitzgerald, F. Scott. *The Great Gatsby.* New York: Charles Scribner's Sons, 1925.
Flaubert, Gustave. *Madame Bovary.* New York: The Modern Library, 1857; 1950.
Foster, David William. *Gay and Lesbian Themes in Latin American Writing.* Austin: University of Texas Press, 1991.
Foster, David William. *Sexual Textualities: Essays on Queer/ing Latin American Writing.* Austin: University of Texas Press, 1997.
Foucault, Michel. *Discipline and Punish: The Birth of the Prison.* New York: Vintage, 1979.
Foucault, Michel. *The History of Sexuality: An Introduction, Volume 1.* New York: Vintage, 1990.
Frank, Gerald. *Judy.* New York: Harper & Row, 1975.
Freud, Sigmund. "Three Contributions to the Theory of Sex." *The Basic Writings of Sigmund Freud.* New York: The Modern Library, 1938.
Freud, Sigmund. *Civilization and its Discontents.* New York: W.W. Norton & Co., 1961.

Fuss, Diana. *Essentially Speaking: Feminism, Nature, and Difference.* New York: Routledge, 1989.
Garber, Marjorie. *Vested Interests: Cross-Dressing and Cultural Anxiety.* New York: Routledge, 1992.
Gazarian-Gautier, Marie-Lise. *Interviews with Latin American Writers.* Elmwood Park, IL: Dalkey Archive Press, 1989.
Goldman, William. *The Season: A Candid Look at Broadway.* New York: Harcourt, Brace & World, Inc., 1969.
Grossberg, Lawrence. *We gotta get out of this place: popular conservatism and postmodern culture.* New York: Routledge, 1992.
Hall, Stuart. *Critical Dialogues in Cultural Studies.* Ed. David Morley and Kuan-Hsing Chen. New York: Routledge, 1996.
Hebdige, Dick. *Subculture: The Meaning of Style.* New York: Routledge, 1979.
Hebdige, Dick. "Postmodernism and 'the other side.'" *Critical Dialogues in Cultural Studies.* Eds. David Morley and Kuan-Hsing Chen. New York: Routledge, 1996.
Islas, Arturo. *The Rain God.* Palo Alto: Alexandrian Press, 1984.
Islas, Arturo. *Migrant Souls.* New York: William Morrow & Co., 1990.
Jameson, Fredric. "Cognitive Mapping." *Marxism and the Interpretation of Culture.* Eds. Cary Nelson and Lawrence Grossberg, Urbana: University of Illinois Press, 1988.
Jameson, Fredric. *Postmodernism, or the Cultural Logic of Late Capitalism.* Durham: Duke University Press, 1991.
Kael, Pauline. *Deeper into Movies.* New York: Warner Books Edition, 1973.
Kael, Pauline. *Reeling.* Boston: Little, Brown and Company, 1976.
Kaiser, Charles. *The Gay Metropolis: 1940–1996.* New York: Houghton Mifflin Co., 1997.
Kulick, Don. *Travesti: Sex, Gender, and Culture among Brazilian Transgendered Prostitutes.* Chicago: University of Chicago Press, 1998.
Laclau, Ernesto and Mouffe, Chantal. *Hegemony and Socialist Struggle: Towards a Radical Democratic Politics.* New York: Verso, 1985.
Leap, William L. *Word's Out: Gay Men's English.* Minneapolis: University of Minnesota Press, 1996.
Lewes, Kenneth. *The Psychoanalytic Theory of Male Homosexuality.* New York: New American Library, 1988.
Limon, Jose E. *Dancing with the Devil: Society and Cultural Poetics in Mexican-American South Texas.* Madison: The University of Wisconsin Press, 1994.
Lumsden, Ian. *Machos, Maricones, and Gays: Cuba and Homosexuality.* Philadelphia: Temple University Press, 1996.
"The Man that Got Away." Ira Gershwin, Harold Arlen.
Maril, Robert Lee. *Poorest of Americans: The Mexican Americans of the Lower Rio Grande Valley of Texas.* Notre Dame: University of Notre Dame Press, 1989.
Memmi, Albert. *The Colonizer and the Colonized.* Boston: Beacon Press, 1967.
Meyer, Michael C. *The Course of Mexican History.* New York: Oxford University Press, 1995.
Moraga, Cherrie. *Love in the War Years.* Boston: South End Press, 1983.
Moraga, Cherrie. *The Last Generation.* Boston: South End Press, 1993.

Munoz, Carlos, Jr. *Youth, Identity, Power: The Chicano Movement*. New York: Verso, 1989.
Murray, Stephen O. "Machismo, Male Homosexuality, and Latino Culture." *Latin American Homosexualities*. Albuquerque: University of New Mexico Press, 1995.
Myer, Moe, ed. *The Politics and Poetics of Camp*. New York: Routledge, 1994.
Newton, Esther. *Mother Camp: Female Impersonators in America*. Chicago: The University of Chicago Press, 1972.
Ngugi, Wa Thiong'O. *Decolonising the Mind: The Politics of Language in African Literature*. London: James Currey, 1986.
Omi, Michael and Winant, Howard. *Racial Formations in the United States*. New York: Routledge, 1994.
"Over the Rainbow." E. Y. Harburg and Vernon Duke.
Prieur, Annick. *Mema's House, Mexico City: On Transvestites, Queens, and Machos*. Chicago: The University of Chicago Press, 1998.
Puig, Manuel. *Betrayed by Rita Hayworth*. New York: Avon Books, 1971.
Puig, Manuel. *Kiss of the Spider Woman*. New York: Vintage, 1991.
Roman, David. "Latino Literature." *The Gay and Lesbian Literary Heritage*. Ed. Claude J. Summers. New York: Henry Holt & Co., 1995.
Ross, Andrew. "The Uses of Camp." *Camp Grounds: Style and Homosexuality*. Ed. David Bergman. Amherst: University of Massachusetts Press, 1993.
Rowe, William and Schelling, Vivian. *Memory and Modernity: Popular Culture in Latin America*. New York: Verso, 1991.
Russo, Vito. *The Celluloid Closet: Homosexuality in the Movies*. New York: Harper & Row, 1987.
Saldívar, Jose David. *The Dialectics of Our America: Geneology, Cultural Critique, and Literary History*. Durham: Duke University Press, 1991.
Saldívar, Ramon. *Chicano Narrative: The Dialectics of Difference*. Madison: University of Wisconsin Press, 1990.
Sedgwick, Eve Kosofsky. *Epistemology of the Closet*. Berkeley: University of California Press, 1990.
Sedgwick, Eve Kosofsky. "Queer Performativity, Henry James' 'The Art of the Novel.' " *GLQ* Vol. 1, No. 1 (1993).
Sedgwick, Eve Kosofsky. *Tendencies*. Durham: Duke University Press, 1994.
Signorile, Michelangelo. *Queer in America: Sex, the Media, and the Closets of Power*. New York: Random House, 1993.
Sontag, Susan. *A Susan Sontag Reader*. New York: Vintage, 1983.
Spector, Nancy. *Felix Gonzalez-Torres*. New York: Solomon R. Guggenheim Museum, 1995.
Tittler, Jonathan. *Manuel Puig*. New York: Twayne Publishers, 1993.
Warner, Michael, ed. *Fear of a Queer Planet: Queer Politics and Social Theory*. Minneapolis: University of Minnesota Press, 1993.

Index

affect, 9, 13, 15, 73, 85
AIDS, 61, 97–8, 100–1, 131, 132, 135
Albee, Edward, 36–7, 42–4, 47
Alvarez Muñoz, Celia, 3–7
American theater and homosexuality, 37–8
Anzaldua, Gloria, 9–11
Arlen, Harold, 87, 90

Bacarisse, Pamela, 102, 104
Barnes, Clive, 25
The Boys in the Band, 23–50, 62, 130, 133, 134
  Albee, Edward, 42
  camp, 23, 25–7, 29–32, 47, 48
  characters, 27–30
  critical responses to, 25–6
  gender identity, 30
  historical context, 24
  the play, 24–5
borderlands, 7, 9–12
  see also Anzaldua, Gloria
Bronski, Michael, 25, 37
Brooks, Peter, 12–13
Burroughs, William S., 19
Butler, Judith, 92, 93, 95, 127

camp
  in American theater, 37–8
  in *The Boys in the Band*, 23, 25–7, 29–32
  definitions of, 2, 23, 27, 41, 77
  drag, 75–8

gender identity, 30, 49, 118
homosexuality, 40–1
  in *Kiss of the Spider Woman*, 104, 114, 117, 127, 129
  language, 30–5
  limitations of, 23–4, 27
  masculinity, 30–1
  as performance, 41–2
  Puig, Manuel, 102
  race, 23, 35–6, 46–7, 49
  sensibility, 2, 49
  sentimentality, 48–9
  stigmatizing effects, 31–5
Canby, Vincent, 94
Cat People, 110–12, 114, 117
Champagne, John, 94–6
Chicana/os
  Catholicism, 57–8, 60, 61, 65, 66, 68
  cockroaches, representations of, 53–4
  as colic coupling, 7
  identity, 51–2
  language, 11–12
  machismo, 57, 61, 128
  narrative, 51–2
  nationalism, 57
  queerness, 9–11, 61
  suffering, representations of, 2, 133–4
  South Texas, 18
  see also borderlands; cultural authenticity
Chicano art, 3

144 / INDEX

Chicano closet, 61–2, 65, 72, 73, 74
Chicano Movement, the, 3
Cisneros, Sandra, 51, 52–60, 133
closet, the, 61–2, 68–71, 78
  see also Chicano closet
Clurman, Harold, 25, 44
Colas, Santiago, 105, 107
colic coupling, 3, 5, 7, 14, 117, 118
coming out, 62, 69–70, 73, 74
Conceptual art, 3, 6, 131
Crowley, Mart, 23–49
  see also The Boys in the Band
cultural authenticity, 53–7

Dada, 6
desire
  cultural identity, 56–7
  melodrama, 58
  narrative, 12–13, 134
  power, 110
drag
  assumptions about, 75–6
  camp, 75–8
  as cross-dressing, 84–5
  definition of, 77
  fantasy, 76, 93–4, 96
  fashion world, 75, 97
  Garland, Judy, 86, 91
  gender identity, 76, 79–81,
    83, 97
  humor, 76, 79
  as performance, 76, 78, 81–3,
    85–6
  in queer culture, 75–7
  race, 76, 92, 95, 96
  spectacle, 75
  stage performers, 81–3
  stardom, 85, 98, 134
  Stonewall, 24
  street fairies, 81–3
  subversion, 95–6
  utopia, 76, 85, 88, 92, 130, 134
Duke, Vernon, 1

Dyer, Richard
  on camp, 49
  on emotional intensity, 134
  on entertainment, 14
  on Garland, Judy, 85, 86, 89–91
  on psychoanalysis, 13–14
  on representation, 6

Fitzgerald, Ella, 1–2
Foucault, Michel, 95, 108–10, 129

Garber, Marjorie, 76, 83–5
Garland, Judy, 20, 25, 27, 76,
  85–91, 134
gender identity
  The Boys in the Band, 30
  drag, 76, 79–81, 83, 97
  Kiss of the Spider Woman, 115–18,
    121–2, 126–7
  Paris is Burning, 92, 93, 96
  race, 92–3
Gershwin, Ira, 90
Goldman, William, 38–9
Gonzalez-Torres, Felix,
  131–3, 135
The Great Gatsby, 18–19
Grossberg, Lawrence, 9, 13, 14–15,
  73, 85
  see also affect

Hall, Stuart, 16
Harburg, E.Y., 1, 87
Hebdige, Dick, 7–8
Hollywood movies, 16–21
hooks, bell, 94–6
Hurt, William, 99–100

identity, 8, 10, 54–6
  coming out, 62
  see also cultural authenticity;
    gender identity
Islas, Arturo, 51, 60–74, 130, 133, 135
  AIDS, 101, 102

autobiography, 63–4, 133
closetedness, 60–4

Jameson, Fredric, 4–5, 52–3

Kael, Pauline, 16–17, 26–7, 45–6
Kaufman, Stanley, 38
Kiss of the Spider Woman, 99–130, 134
   camp, 104, 114, 117–18, 123, 127, 129
   characters, relationships of, 105–6, 112–16, 124–6, 128–9
   effeminacy, 102–4
   film version, 99–100
   gender identity, 115–18, 121–2, 126–7
   Hollywood movies, 110, 116–17, 129
   masculinity, 121–2, 126–8
   politics, 105
   power, *see*, Foucault, Michel
   seduction, 114
   transformations, 117–18, 120, 123, 128–9
   see also Cat People; Nazi propaganda film

Latino gay texts, lack of, 61
Leap, William L., 30–1

"The Man That Got Away", *see, A Star is Born*
Manrique, Jaime, 100–1
melodrama, 2, 46, 58
Moraga, Cherrie, 11, 57, 61–2
Murray, Stephen, 128

Nazi propaganda film, 110–11, 118–21, 123
New Queer Cinema, 91
   see also Paris is Burning

Newton, Esther
   camp and homosexuality, 40, 43, 77–8, 118
   camp humor, 79
   drag and queer theory, 76, 85
   drag, types of, 81–3
   gender identity, 79–81

"Over the Rainbow", *see The Wizard of Oz* race, as relates to:
   camp, 23, 35–6, 46–7, 49
   class, 55
   cultural authenticity, 133
   drag, 76, 92, 96
   gender, 56, 57
   gender identity, 92–3
   queerness, 10, 91
   religion, 57–8
   sexuality, 9, 74, 91, 98; *see also* Chicano closet
   utopia, 98, 133

Paris is Burning, 76, 85, 91–8, 118, 134
   critical responses to, 94–6
   fashion world, 97
   gender identity, 92, 93, 96
   New Queer Cinema, 91
   race, 93–7
   popular culture, liberating power of, 15–16, 58, 134
postmodernism, 7–8, 8–9, 52–3
power, *see* Foucault, Michel
Puig, Manuel, 99–102, 134, 135
   camp, 102
   childhood, 102
   death, 100–1
   film version, reaction to, 100
   homosexuality, 100–1
   see also Kiss of the Spider Woman

queer, 7, 10, 12, 91
Queer Theory, relationship with drag, 75–6

Ross, Andrew, 39
Russo, Vito, 26–8, 67

Saldívar, Jose David, 63
Saldívar, Ramon, 51
Sedgwick, Eve Kosofsky, 10, 51, 69–70
Sontag, Susan, 39–43, 48–9, 53
A Star is Born, 25, 89–91
Stonewall, 24, 49, 75, 83, 91
suffering in love, *see*, unrequited love
Surrealism, 6

telenovelas, 17, 58–9, 133
transvestite, 84–5
Tuttle, Jonathan, 101

unrequited love
 in *The Boys in the Band*, 46–7
 definition, 15–16
 in *The Great Gatsby*, 18–19
 Hollywood movies, 21
 humiliation, 44, 47
 identity, 60

as recovery, 16
suffering in love, 2–3, 58–60, 64, 66, 73, 133–4
utopia, 2, 16, 21, 129, 135
utopia
 in art, 132–3, 135
 defined, 2
 drag, 76, 85, 88, 92, 130, 134
 entertainment as, 106–7
 Hollywood movies, 16
 impulses, 6
 loss, 133
 popular culture, 134
 in prison cell, 105–10, 129
 race, 98, 133
 revolution as, 107
 unrequited love, 2, 16, 21, 129, 135

voguing, 92, 93

Williams, Tennessee, 20, 36–7, 42
The Wizard of Oz, 87–9